ILLUSTRATED ENCYCLOPEDIA OF

SCIENCE

—— AND ——

TECHNOLOGY

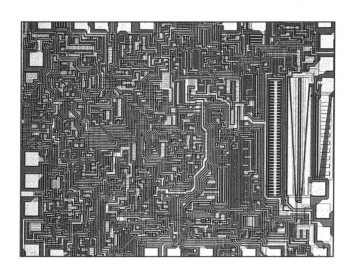

This book is a compilation of sections from *Journey Through Inventions* by Ron Taylor,
Journey Through Science by Douglas McTavish, and *Journey Through Space* by Tim Furniss,
all published by Hamlyn Children's Books.

This compilation first published by Dean, an imprint of
Reed Children's Books, Michelin House, 81 Fulham Road,
London SW3 6RB and Auckland, Melbourne, Singapore and Toronto.

ISBN 0 603 55410 5

British Library Cataloguing-in-Publication Data.
A catalogue record for this book is available from the British Library.

Printed in Italy

ILLUSTRATED ENCYCLOPEDIA OF
SCIENCE
— AND —
TECHNOLOGY

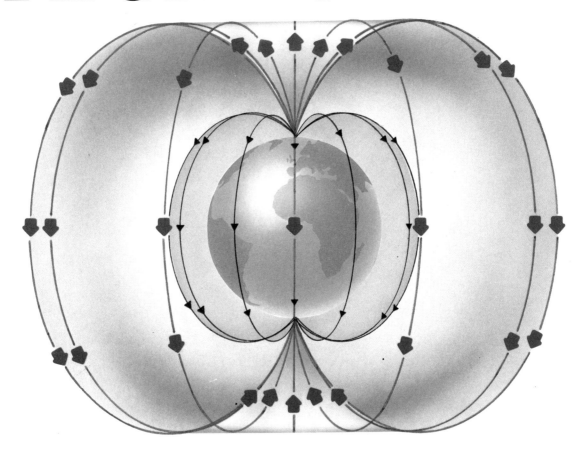

TIM FURNISS,
DOUGLAS McTAVISH,
RON TAYLOR

DEAN

CONTENTS

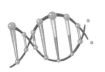    

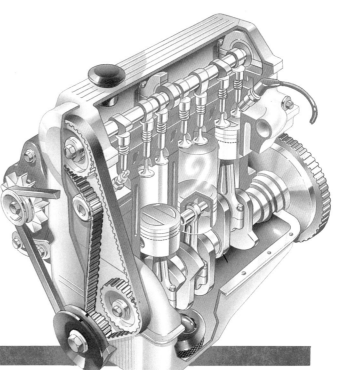

THE
PHYSICAL
WORLD

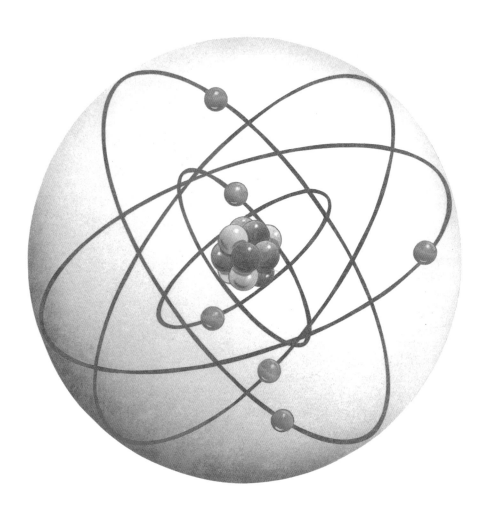

THE NATURE OF MATTER

Everything on earth and in the universe around us consists of what we call matter. All matter is made up of tiny building blocks called atoms, which sometimes join together in groups called molecules. These atoms and molecules also join together to form elements and compounds. An element contains atoms of just one type - pure gold, for example, contains only gold atoms. Compounds are combinations of different elements, and so they are made from atoms of two or more types. Common salt is a compound made by mixing sodium and chlorine atoms.

In any substance, each atom or molecule is attracted to the other atoms and molecules around it by what are called electromagnetic forces. If you rest your elbow on something hard, such as a table, your arm does not sink in because these forces hold the atoms in the table close together.

However, atoms and molecules are moving all the time. They vibrate constantly, travelling a tiny distance in one direction, then in another, and so on. Sometimes they move faster and sometimes slower, and the forces between them can become weaker or stronger; when these factors change, the way in which matter behaves changes too.

Solids, Liquids and Gases

Matter takes many forms, but it comes in three basic states - solid, liquid and gas. In a solid, the atoms or molecules are vibrating relatively slowly. Also, they are very close together and the forces between them are strong. This is what gives many solids their strength and hardness. Solids in which the forces are weak are not as hard as those with strong forces. Examples of this are diamond and graphite (the "lead" in pencils), both of which are solids made up of carbon atoms. In diamond, an extremely hard material, the forces between the atoms are very strong. In graphite, however, the carbon atoms are in layers which lie one on top of another. The forces between layers are not very strong and the layers can slide over each other quite easily, which makes graphite weak.

Diamond, graphite and most other solids are made up of crystals - small pieces of material with straight edges and flat sides. Sugar and salt are well-known crystals. If you looked through a powerful microscope at steel you would see that it, too, consists of crystals.

The forces between atoms or molecules in a liquid are weaker than those in a solid. Because of this, liquids can flow from place to place. However, the forces are strong enough to resist flow, and this resistance is called viscosity. Liquids with high viscosity, such as treacle, flow slowly while those with low viscosity, such as water, flow more quickly.

Unlike solids, liquids do not have a definite shape - they take the shape of whatever container they are in. When a liquid is still, its surface is perfectly level. Another property of liquids is that some substances, including solids, gases and other liquids, will dissolve in them, forming what are called solutions.

Below: When steel is magnified hundreds of times, we can see that it is made up of crystals.

EVERYTHING IS MADE OF MATTER, WHICH CONSISTS OF ATOMS AND MOLECULES

The atoms or molecules in a gas are vibrating extremely fast, so fast that the forces between them cannot hold them together. Many gases, including air, are impossible to see because their molecules are far apart. They are also very easy to compress, or squeeze. Like liquids, gases can flow, but other substances will not dissolve in them. One gas will mix with another in a process called diffusion.

Changing State

Some substances are familiar to us in all three states. Water is a good example; normally it is a liquid, but we also know it as a solid, ice, and as a gas, steam. The state it is in depends upon the temperature. It becomes solid when we cool it down to 0°C and turns into a gas when heated to 100°C. When water is heated, the molecules move faster and faster until, at 100°C (boiling point), they break the forces between them and the water becomes a gas. When cooled, the molecules vibrate slower and slower until, at 0°C (freezing point), the forces between them are strong enough to hold the water together as a solid. Many other substances can be made to change state by heating or cooling them.

Below: Whether a substance is solid, liquid or gaseous depends on the amount of energy its atoms or molecules contain.

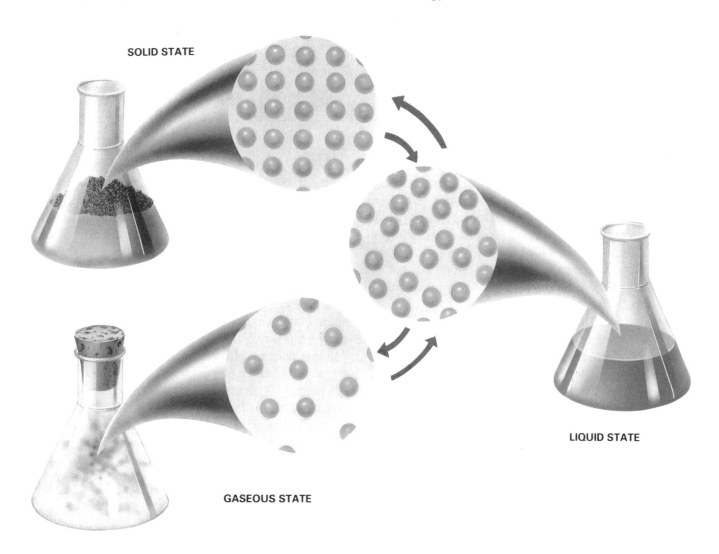

SOLID STATE

GASEOUS STATE

LIQUID STATE

INSIDE THE ATOM

Since the time of the ancient Greeks, many scientists have believed that all matter is made up of atoms. However, the first real evidence that atoms actually exist did not come until 1802. In that year, the Englishman John Dalton was able to measure the mass of certain atoms and to explain how they joined together to form molecules. Like the Greeks, Dalton thought atoms were the smallest particles that could exist, and he pictured them as being like very small billiard balls.

Christmas Puddings, Clouds and Shells

In 1897 another English scientist, J. J. Thomson, suggested that atoms contained even smaller particles, called electrons, dotted about like currants in a Christmas pudding. Some years later Ernest Rutherford showed that all atoms contained electrons, which he thought circled in a cloud around a dense region at the centre, called the nucleus. In 1913 Neils Bohr said that the electrons orbited around the nucleus in a series of layers, or shells, rather like planets circling the Sun.

In fact, the paths followed by electrons as they fly around the nucleus of an atom are much more complicated than Bohr imagined. When electrons are passed through a narrow slit they appear to spread out in a wave. This means that, inside an atom, it is impossible to predict exactly where an electron might be at any moment. So, instead of placing them in precise orbits, scientists now draw three-dimensional maps of electron "orbitals" showing where they are likely to be. The four simplest orbital shapes are a sphere, a dumb-bell, a four-leaf clover, and an hourglass and ring. Others are too complicated to draw.

Inside the Nucleus

The proton, one of the building blocks which make up the nucleus, was first discovered in 1886. Each proton carries a positive electric charge, and the number of protons in an atom is balanced by an equal number of negatively charged electrons. The next particle to be discovered inside the nucleus was the neutron, which was identified by James Chadwick in 1932. Neutrons have no electric charge. Other particles have since been discovered using what are called particle accelerators. Inside these machines, particles such as electrons and neutrons are accelerated to very high speeds and fired at atomic nuclei. If an accelerated particle scores a direct hit on a nucleus, other particles are produced. These new particles can survive for only a very short time, and so the tracks they make must be recorded very

DALTON'S THEORY 1802 • ELECTRON 1897 • PROTON 1886 • EINSTEIN'S PHOTON 1905

ELECTRON ORBITALS

When electrons were first discovered, scientists thought that these tiny particles moved around the nuclei of atoms in a sort of cloud, or that they orbited in layers. In fact, the exact path of an electron is far too complex to work out. Modern scientists use three-dimensional maps to show electron orbitals - regions in which electrons are likely to be found. These are the four simplest orbital shapes: there are others that are so complicated they are almost impossible to draw.

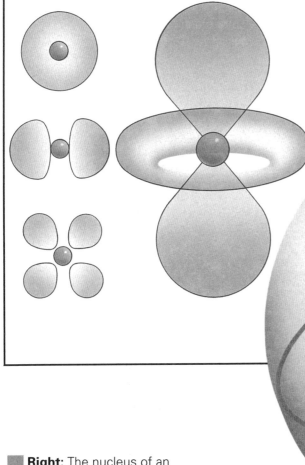

quickly using special detectors.

New particles found in this way include muons, taus, and neutrinos (known collectively as leptons), pions and kaons (so-called composite particles) and quarks. It seems that protons, neutrons and some other composite particles are made up of a number of quarks. There are now thought to be six different types of quark, which have been christened Up, Down, Strange, Charm, Bottom and Top.

As well as these leptons, quarks and composite particles, there is another group called bosons. One of them, the photon, is a particle of light which was first suggested by Albert Einstein in 1905. Another boson is called the gluon; experiments carried out in 1982 seem to prove their existence but they have never been seen. Even more mysterious are gravitons, which are thought to be gravity particles although there is, as yet, no evidence that they exist.

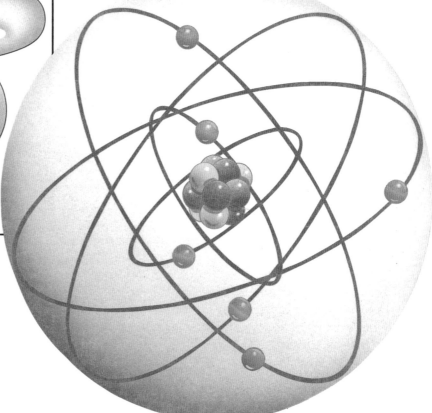

Right: The nucleus of an atom consists of protons and neutrons. Electrons orbit around the nucleus. This is a carbon atom, with 6 electrons and 6 protons.

FORCES AND MOTION

A force is something that affects the shape and motion of an object. There are four main types of force: electric, magnetic, nuclear and gravitational. Electric force acts between two electrically charged particles (pp. 10-11). A force between two moving electric charges is called a magnetic force (pp. 46-47). (The electromagnetic forces which hold atoms and molecules together are a combination of these two forces.) Nuclear forces exist between the tiny particles inside the nucleus of an atom (pp. 10-11). Gravitational force is the attraction between any two objects which have mass (pp. 14-15). When you push or pull an object you are applying a force; this type of force is related to gravitational force.

The study of the relationship between the motion of an object and the forces acting upon it is called dynamics. Among the first people to think about the way in which things move, and why, were the ancient Greeks, whose civilization was at its height between the sixth and third centuries BC. They believed that every object in the universe had its own special place, and that things moved to get back to where they belonged. The natural place for rocks to be was on the earth, so if one was lifted up and dropped it would fall downwards.

Galileo and Newton

The teachings of the Greeks, especially those of a man called Aristotle, went unchallenged for almost 2,000 years. In 1591, a scientist called Galileo Galilei discovered that objects move simply because they are pushed or pulled by forces.

Galileo did not know what the forces are. The problem was solved in 1687 by Isaac Newton. In his book, *Principia*, he set out his three laws of motion which explained how forces act to make things move. He also showed that one special force, gravitation, acted throughout the whole Universe (see the chapter on Gravity). In honour of this great scientist's work, all forces are now measured in units called newtons.

Friction and Centripetal Force

When you kick a ball across the ground, it doesn't carry on moving for ever. It slows down gradually and eventually stops. From Newton's laws of motion we know that this is because there is a force acting on the ball causing it to slow down. This force is called friction and it acts when two surfaces rub together. Without the friction between our feet and the ground we would not be able to walk along.

If you tie a conker at one end of a length of string and whirl it around your head, it follows a circular path. The direction in which it moves changes all the time which, according to Newton, means that a force must be acting upon it. This force acts through the string. If the string broke, the force would stop acting and the conker would fly off through the air in a straight line. The force that causes the circular motion of the conker is called centripetal force, and it acts towards the centre of the circle. It is sometimes, though mistakenly, called centrifugal force.

Below: Centripetal force keeps this athlete's hammer moving in a circle.

NEWTON'S LAWS OF MOTION

The First Law of Motion states that an object will stay still or continue moving at the same speed in a straight line unless a force acts upon it. This idea, first suggested by Galileo, is called inertia. A large ship such as an oil tanker, moving at a steady speed, has so much inertia that it must begin slowing down a long way before it needs to stop.

Newton's Second Law says that a moving object moves faster, or accelerates, when acted on by a force. It accelerates in the direction of the force, and the amount of acceleration depends on the size of the force and the mass of the object - how much matter it contains. That is why a heavy stone is more difficult to throw than a lighter one.

The Third Law of Motion says that forces act in pairs. When you push or pull an object, it pushes or pulls back with an equal force. Athletes take advantage of this when they use starting blocks for races; when they push against the blocks, the blocks push back with an equal force, and propel the runners forward.

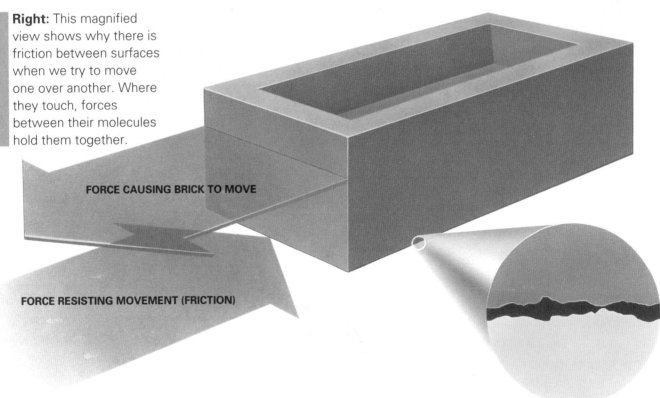

Right: This magnified view shows why there is friction between surfaces when we try to move one over another. Where they touch, forces between their molecules hold them together.

FORCE CAUSING BRICK TO MOVE

FORCE RESISTING MOVEMENT (FRICTION)

GRAVITY

Why is it that we are able to walk around the Earth without flying off into space? Why doesn't the Moon crash into our planet or veer off into the universe? To the ancient Greeks, the answer was clear: humans, the Moon and the Earth are all in their natural places.

Newton and Universal Gravitation

Galileo's experiments of the 1590s told him that objects moved when forces acted upon them, but he didn't know what the forces were. As we have seen, the problem was solved by Isaac Newton. It is said that he was sitting in an orchard one day when an apple fell to the ground. He realized that the Earth must be pulling the apple towards it. This started him thinking about other objects in the universe, and he calculated that they were all attracted to each other by a single force, gravity. It is gravity that holds the Moon in its orbit and keeps us on the surface of the Earth. Gravity is what gives us weight. We all have mass - the more matter we contain,

the greater is our mass. Weight is the downward force which is exerted on us by gravity, and so the more mass we have, the more we weigh.

Newton's studies showed that if you travel away from the Earth, the force of gravity gradually becomes weaker. This is because the gravitational pull between two objects depends upon how far apart they are. In fact, gravity decreases as the square of the distance between the objects increases, so if you double the distance, the pull between them is one quarter of what

Below: Isaac Newton may have first thought about gravity when he watched an apple fall from a tree.

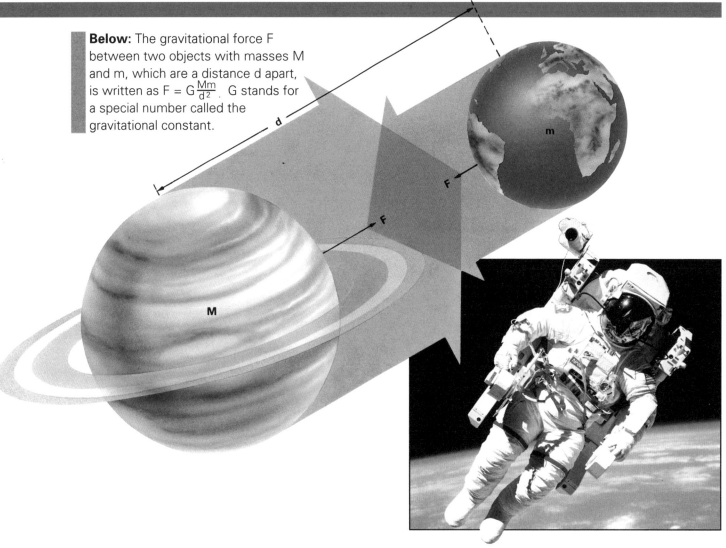

Below: The gravitational force F between two objects with masses M and m, which are a distance d apart, is written as $F = G\frac{Mm}{d^2}$. G stands for a special number called the gravitational constant.

Above: A person on the Moon experiences less gravitational force than on the Earth.

it was originally. As we have seen, gravitational attraction is also affected by the mass of the objects. Because the Moon's mass is only one sixth as much as the Earth's, its gravitational pull is one-sixth of that on Earth. If you can jump 1 m into the air on Earth, you would be able to jump 6 m on the Moon.

Einstein and Gravitational Waves

In 1915 a German-born scientist, Albert Einstein, published his General Theory of Relativity. According to this theory, the force of gravity is different from the other types of force we experience on Earth. Einstein said that the vast area of space, in which the stars and planets exist, is not the same everywhere. In some places around stars with a very high mass space is actually curved, and this is what causes gravity. For example, the Sun curves the space around it and forces the Earth to travel along a curved path.

In Einstein's theory the attraction between two bodies, such as the Earth and the Sun, moves in waves. These gravitational waves are very weak and no one has yet been able to prove they exist on Earth. However, when astronomers looked closely at a large star far out in space, called PSR 1913+ 16, they were able to show that it was giving off gravitational waves. Thanks to these observations and other experiments, the General Theory of Relativity is now accepted by most scientists.

FLUIDS

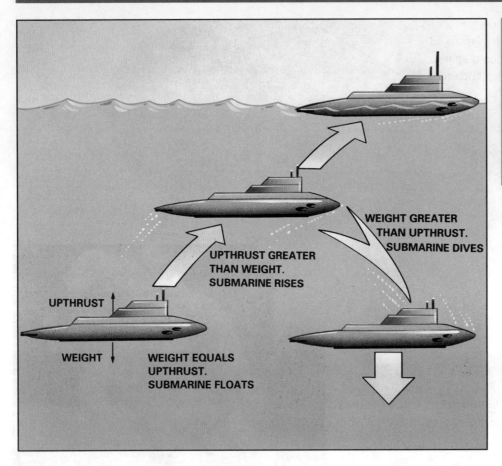

UPTHRUST GREATER
THAN WEIGHT.
SUBMARINE RISES

WEIGHT GREATER
THAN UPTHRUST.
SUBMARINE DIVES

UPTHRUST

WEIGHT

WEIGHT EQUALS
UPTHRUST.
SUBMARINE FLOATS

Left: When the weight of a submarine is equal to the upthrust on it, the submarine floats underwater. When it is heavier it sinks, and when it is lighter, it rises. The weight is adjusted by changing the amounts of air and water in its ballast tanks.

Have you ever noticed that you feel lighter when you are in the bath? This is because you actually weigh less when you are immersed in water, even though your mass remains exactly the same as it was before you got into the bath.

Archimedes' Principle

The first person to think about this was a Greek scientist called Archimedes, who lived more than 2,000 years ago. He discovered that when an object is placed in a fluid (a liquid or a gas) it displaces or moves aside some of the fluid, and the object's weight is reduced. The apparent loss in weight is equal to the weight of the displaced fluid.

A person in a bath or any other solid object immersed in a fluid weighs less than in the air because the water pushes up on them with what is called an upthrust. To put Archimedes' Principle another way, the upthrust on an object is equal to the weight of fluid it displaces.

Pressure, Density and Surface Tension

The upthrust on an immersed object is caused by pressure within the fluid. Pressure is the force acting upon the object divided by the area of the object. The deeper you go in a fluid, the greater the pressure, so the pressure at the bottom of an immersed object is higher than at the top. The difference in pressure produces an upthrust on the object.

The pressure in a fluid also depends upon the density of the fluid: its weight divided by its volume (the amount of space it takes up). A litre of air weighs much less than a litre of water, so we say that air is less dense than water. If an object is placed in a fluid that is more dense, it will float. For example, ice is only about nine-tenths as dense as water, so an ice cube floats with about 90 per cent of it underwater.

The air around us is a fluid and so it exerts a pressure, which we call atmospheric pressure. One of the first people to prove this was Evangelista Torricelli who, in

ARCHIMEDES (287-212 BC) DISCOVERS PRINCIPLE OF FLOATING OBJECTS

1643, invented a device called a barometer in which atmospheric pressure forced mercury to rise inside a glass tube. The height to which it rose depended upon the pressure of the atmosphere. As we know, pressure varies with depth, and so the atmospheric pressure at the earth's surface - at the bottom of the atmosphere - is greater than at the top of a mountain.

There are many animals that can float in water, and some that can even walk on it. Small insects, such as pond skaters, are able to walk across the surface of a pond without getting their feet wet. They can do this because of something called surface tension.

Water is made up of molecules, held together by forces between them. At the surface, this causes water to act almost as though it is covered with a thin rubber skin. The surface tension is strong enough to support the weight of pond skaters. It also explains why rain falls in rounded drops; the molecules nearest the outside of the drops are pulled inwards towards the centre of the liquid.

Right: We feel lighter in a fluid because of the upward force, or upthrust, exerted by the fluid.

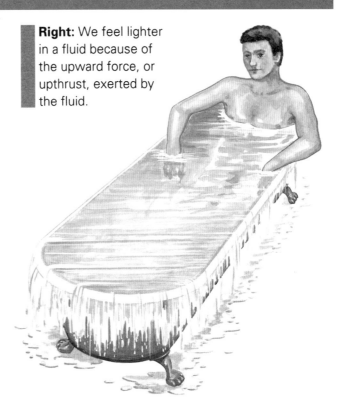

Below: Water flowing from holes in a cylinder shows how pressure in a fluid increases with depth.

Below: Although it is more dense than water, this razor blade "floats" because of surface tension.

ATMOSPHERIC PRESSURE ON EARTH IS 76 CM OF MERCURY

ELASTICITY

If you hold a rubber band with both hands and pull it, the band stretches and then returns to its normal length when you stop pulling it. However, if you pull hard enough the band will eventually break.

The same thing happens when a weight is hung from the end of a length of wire. At first, the wire stretches slightly, but it returns to normal when the weight is removed. This is called elastic stretching. If a heavier weight is used, the wire will stretch but will not return to normal. If the weight is increased even more, the wire will become what is called "plastic", and will stretch very rapidly and then break.

Hooke's Law

In 1676 an English scientist, Robert Hooke, discovered the law that governs the way in which solid materials stretch. He found that the amount of stretching, or extension, of a wire is directly linked to the weight attached to it, but only up to a certain point. If the weight is increased beyond that point, called the elastic limit, the wire will not return to its normal length but will stay stretched.

It is sometimes very important to know what the elastic limit of a material is. Suspension bridges are often held up by thick wires hung from curved metal

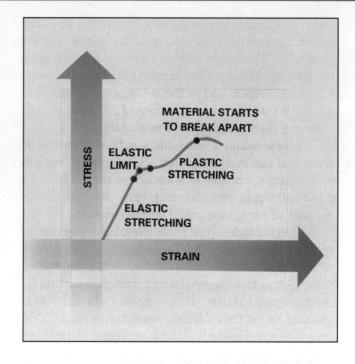

Above: A graph of the stress (force) on a material against strain (how much it stretches). | **Below:** The wires of a suspension bridge must be able to carry a heavy load.

HOOKE'S LAW 1676 • STRETCHING INVOLVES PULLING ATOMS AWAY FROM EACH OTHER

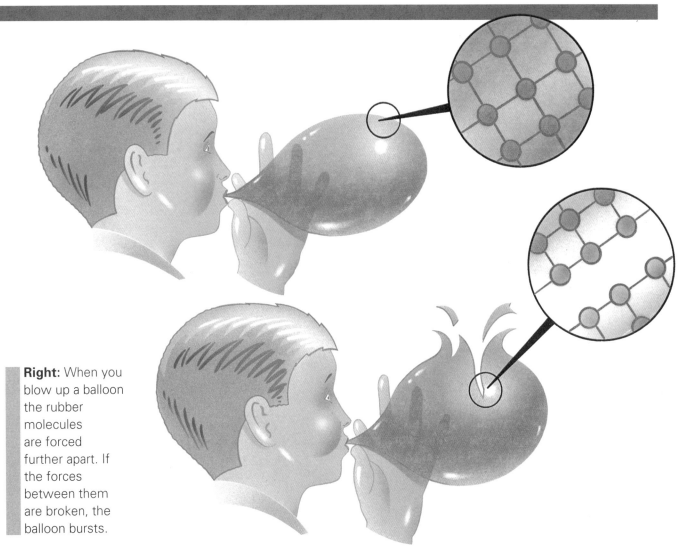

Right: When you blow up a balloon the rubber molecules are forced further apart. If the forces between them are broken, the balloon bursts.

rods that are attached to the tall towers at each end. The engineers who design these bridges have to know that the wires will be strong enough to bear the weight of the bridge and all the traffic it will carry.

Elasticity and Atoms

As we know, all materials are made up of atoms and molecules which are held together by electromagnetic forces. These forces are stronger in solids than in liquids or gases, but it is still possible to weaken them and pull the atoms apart. If you press too hard when you are writing with a pencil, you will break the point. The force you apply on the point is greater than the force holding the atoms together, and so the atoms separate and the "lead" breaks.

When a wire is stretched by a weight, what is really happening is the atoms in the wire are being pulled apart. If the wire isn't stretched too far, the forces between the atoms will pull them back together when the weight is removed. But if it is stretched beyond its elastic limit, the forces are made permanently weaker, and the atoms stay further apart. As a result, the wire remains longer than it was before being stretched. When the wire undergoes elastic stretching, the atoms are actually sliding over one another quite quickly.

All solids can be stretched but some won't stretch very far and they break shortly after their elastic limit is reached. Substances like this, such as glass, are called brittle. In contrast, some substances, such as copper, will stretch a long way beyond their elastic limit before breaking; they are called ductile substances.

MACHINES

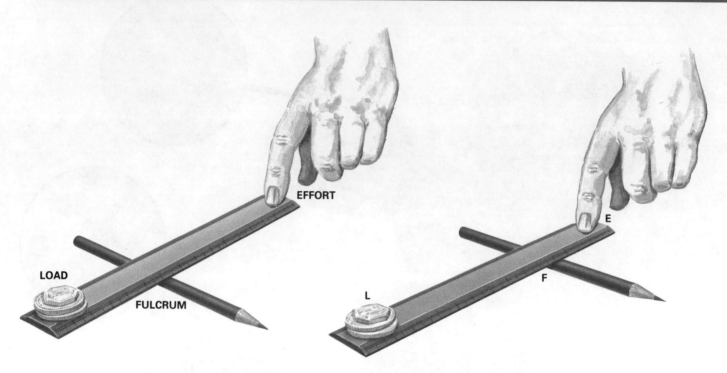

LOAD   EFFORT   FULCRUM

L   E   F

A machine is any device which is used to overcome a force. The force to be overcome is called the load, and when it is applied at one point the machine works by the application of another force, which is called the effort, applied at a different point. There are several different types of machines, including levers, pulleys, wheels and axles, wedges, inclined planes and screws.

Levers and Pulleys

A lever is a rigid object which pivots about a turning point, called the fulcrum, which does not move. If you lay a pencil on a table and rest a ruler across it, you have made a simple lever. The point where the ruler touches the pencil is the fulcrum. You can lift a weight (the load) placed on one end of the ruler by pushing down (applying an effort) on the other end.

Try moving the fulcrum closer to the load; you will find that less effort is needed to lift the load. If the fulcrum is close to the point where you apply the effort, the load is harder to lift. This is because the forces increase with their distance from the fulcrum. So, the longer the distance between the effort and the fulcrum, the greater the load that can be lifted. The Greek scientist Archimedes once said that if he had a long enough lever he could move the earth!

Above: A simple lever. An effort applied at one end can be used to lift a load at the other. Move the fulcrum to see what effect it has on the effort needed to lift the load.

When our ancient ancestors built monuments such as Stonehenge, they probably moved the enormous stones into position using strong logs as levers. Levers that are used every day include scissors, bottle openers and wheelbarrows.

We give levers different names depending upon where the fulcrum is and where the load and effort are applied. In a first-class lever, such as a crowbar, a pair of scissors or a seesaw, the effort and load are on opposite sides of the fulcrum. In a second-class lever, like a wheelbarrow or a bottle opener, the fulcrum is at one end and the load is closer to it than the effort. The fulcrum of a third-class lever, such as a pair of sugar tongs, is also at one end, but the effort is closer to the fulcrum than the load.

A pulley is another type of machine that can be used to lift loads. A string is wound over one or more pulley wheels, and when it is pulled a load is lifted. In most

cases, the more pulley wheels there are, the greater the load that can be lifted with the same effort.

Other Simple Machines

A wheel and axle is a machine used for supplying a turning force. A doorknob is one example. When a small force is applied to the knob, which moves around the axle in a circle, a much larger force is produced on the shaft which turns in a small circle.

An inclined plane is another type of machine. It is much easier to push a heavy object up a sloping plank than to lift it vertically. Logs can be split in half by hammering in a wedge - a machine which applies forces that push sideways.

Some major lifting tasks, such as raising a car to fit a new wheel, can be done using a screw jack. Turning the handle on the jack turns a screw to raise a load. Each complete turn of the handle lifts the load a distance known as the pitch, which is the distance between each thread on the screw.

Below: This type of pulley system, known as a block and tackle, is often used to lift heavy objects. It has several pulley wheels.

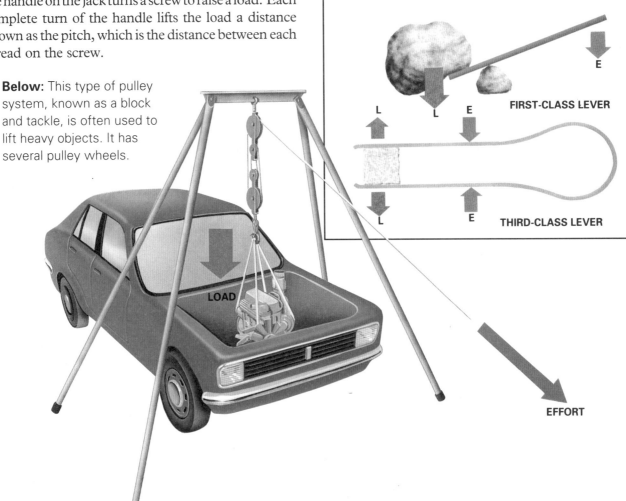

LEVERS

Levers are known as first-, second- or third-class depending upon the position of the fulcrum (the point about which the lever pivots) and the points at which the load (L) and effort (E) are applied. These illustrations show examples of the three classes of levers and how they work.

SECOND-CLASS LEVER

FIRST-CLASS LEVER

THIRD-CLASS LEVER

LOAD

EFFORT

ENERGY

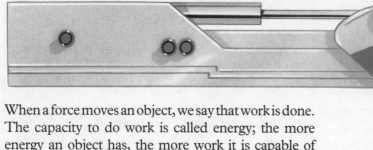

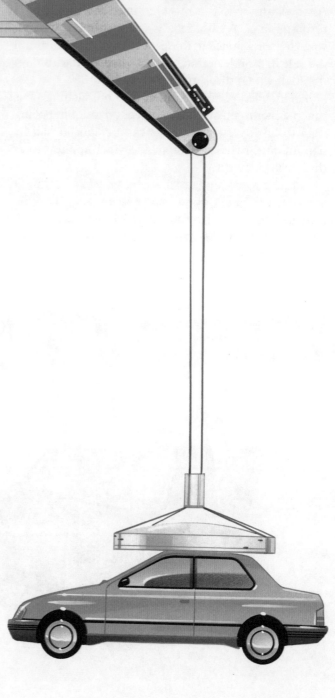
Below: Lifting an object raises its gravitational potential energy.

When a force moves an object, we say that work is done. The capacity to do work is called energy; the more energy an object has, the more work it is capable of doing. Energy exists in many different forms and it can be changed from one form to another, but it can never be created or destroyed. When work is done on or by an object, that object gains or loses energy but the "system" as a whole retains the same amount of energy. For example, if you throw a ball through the air you give it energy, but that energy has come from you and so you have less energy as a result. The system (you and the ball) has exactly the same amount of energy as it had before you threw the ball. Both work and energy are measured in units called joules.

Types of Energy

Scientists group all the different forms of energy into two types: potential energy and kinetic energy. Potential energy is the energy stored in an object or system because of its position, shape or state. The object or system possesses energy because work has been done on it to get it into that position, shape or state.

There are three forms of potential energy. The first of these, gravitational potential energy, is the energy an object has because of its position relative to another object which exerts a gravitational force upon it. If you pick up a stone from the ground, you are giving it gravitational potential energy because the stone is attracted by the earth's gravity. The higher you lift it, the more energy it has.

The second form, electromagnetic potential energy, is the energy of a body associated with its position relative to an electromagnetic force. An example of this is molecular potential energy, which is due to the positions of molecules relative to one another. If two molecules are moved further apart, work is done against the electromagnetic force holding them together, and so their molecular potential energy increases. Elastic potential energy, which is increased when you stretch something such as a rubber band, is a type of molecular

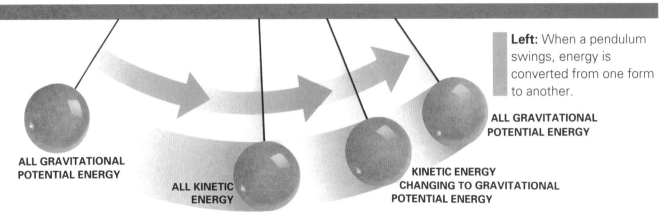

ALL GRAVITATIONAL
POTENTIAL ENERGY

ALL KINETIC
ENERGY

KINETIC ENERGY
CHANGING TO GRAVITATIONAL
POTENTIAL ENERGY

ALL GRAVITATIONAL
POTENTIAL ENERGY

Left: When a pendulum swings, energy is converted from one form to another.

potential energy. Another example of electromagnetic potential energy is chemical energy - the energy stored in fuels and food which is released during chemical reactions, such as when fuel burns or food is digested (see the chapters on Elements and Compounds).

The third form of potential energy is called nuclear potential energy. It is the energy stored inside the nucleus of an atom, and is released during radioactive decay (pp. 50-51) and in nuclear fission and fusion (pp. 52-53).

The other main type of energy kinetic energy is associated with the movement of objects. Kinetic energy can be translational (moving from one place to another), rotational (spinning round), or vibrational (vibrating to and fro).

Energy Conversion

In many cases, objects have more than one type of energy at any one time. Imagine a swinging pendulum, for example. At the top of its swing, when it stops moving, it has gravitational potential energy and no kinetic energy; but when it starts to move downwards more and more of its energy is converted into kinetic energy, which reaches a maximum at the bottom of the swing. As it moves upwards again it slows down as kinetic energy is converted back into gravitational potential energy. The sum of an object's gravitational potential energy and its kinetic energy is called mechanical energy.

As we know, the atoms and molecules inside an object are always moving. They have both kinetic energy and molecular potential energy. The total energy (of both these types) of all of the atoms and molecules in an object is called the internal energy, or thermal energy.

Below: Rocket engines change chemical energy in fuel to kinetic and gravitational potential energy.

ENERGY CAN BE CONVERTED, BUT NOT CREATED OR DESTROYED

HEAT

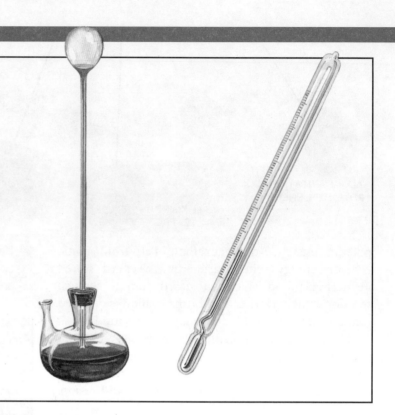

THERMOMETERS

We use thermometers to measure the temperature of things - that is, how hot they are. The device on the left is one of the first ever thermometers, the so-called thermoscope invented by Galileo in the early seventeenth century. It worked on the principle that air expands when it is heated. The clinical thermometer on the right contains mercury instead of air. It is more accurate than Galileo's thermoscope because, when heated, mercury expands more than air. The kink near the bottom of the mercury tube stops the mercury from running back into the bulb before the temperature can be read.

In the previous chapter we looked at energy and some of the forms in which it exists. One of the commonest forms of energy is heat.

Heat and Temperature

There is an important difference between heat and temperature. Temperature is a measure of the hotness or coldness of an object. Heat is the form of energy that flows from one place to another when there is a difference in temperature. When an object is heated its molecules are made to vibrate more rapidly; the heat energy is absorbed by the object and converted into kinetic energy. In this way the object's internal energy - the total energy of all its molecules - is increased. The amount of heat energy a body has depends upon the amount of matter it contains and on its temperature. Therefore, a large, cold object may contain more heat than a small, hot one.

We use thermometers to measure the temperature of things. The thermometer was invented around 1600. We do not know who made the first one, but Galileo certainly produced an air thermometer which he called a thermoscope. It worked on the principle that air (like most other things) expands and takes up more space as it becomes hotter. The first medical thermometer was made in 1626 by an Italian doctor, Santorio. The design was improved in 1867 by Thomas Allbutt. He used mercury as the liquid inside his thermometer, because it expands more than the water Santorio had used, making it easier to read accurately.

Temperature is measured in three scales. On the centigrade, or Celsius, scale, the temperature at which water freezes is 0°C, and that at which it boils is 100°C. On the Fahrenheit scale the freezing and boiling points of water are 32°F and 212°F. The lowest possible temperature on the Kelvin scale is zero Kelvin (0 K), or absolute zero. Scientists think that at this temperature all the molecules in an object stop moving, although no one has ever been able to cool anything down this far. One Kelvin is the same as 1°C; 0°C is 273 K on the Kelvin scale and 100°C is 373 K.

Heat is measured in units called calories. One calorie is the amount of heat needed to warm 1g of water through 1°C.

Latent Heat and Specific Heat Capacity

When an object melts or boils, it takes in heat but its temperature does not rise. Likewise, when it condenses or freezes it gives out heat without its temperature falling. This happens because when an object changes

state the energy it takes in or gives out is used to make or break the electromagnetic forces between the molecules. The heat energy taken in or given out when objects change state without changing their temperature is called latent heat. It was discovered in about 1763 by two scientists, Joseph Black and Johan Wilcke, working independently of each other.

The same two also studied what we call specific heat capacity. When hot objects made of different materials are dropped into cold water, they do not cause the temperature of the water to rise by the same amount even if they have the same mass and are at the same temperature to start with. For example, 100g of glass at 100°C gives out only one-fifth as much heat energy as 100g of water at the same temperature. The specific heat of water was set at 1 to give a standard by which other materials could be measured. So the specific heat of glass is one-fifth of that, or 0.2. This is caused by differering amounts of kinetic and molecular potential energy possessed by molecules in different substances.

Above: Joseph Black (1728-99), the Scottish chemist who discovered the principle of latent heat. Latent means "hidden".

Below: When a substance changes state from solid to liquid or liquid to gas, it takes in heat, but its temperature does not change.

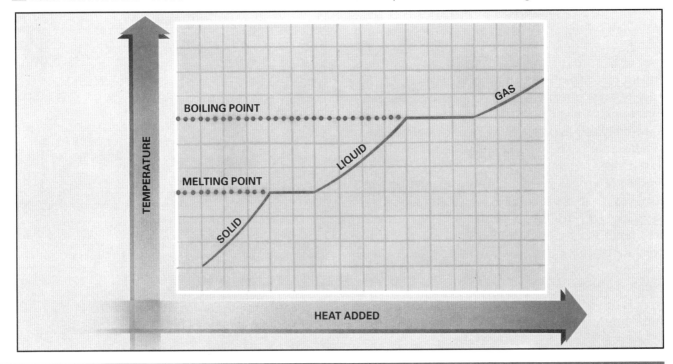

GASES

In a gas, the molecules are travelling extremely fast at about 1,600 km/h. They do not move very far because they are constantly bumping into one another.

The molecules are far too small for us to see, but we can sometimes see the effects of the collisions between them. If smoke particles in the air are studied under a microscope, they can be seen to make small, jerky movements. This motion, called Brownian motion after Robert Brown who first saw it in 1827, is caused by air molecules bumping into the smoke particles and pushing them in all directions.

Boyle's Law and Charles's Law

Gases are easy to squeeze together, or compress, because there is quite a lot of space between their molecules. In 1660 an Irish scientist, Robert Boyle, discovered that if a gas is squeezed so that the pressure on it is doubled, the space it occupies, its volume, is halved. If the volume of a set mass of gas is multiplied by its pressure, the result will always be the same.

Boyle's Law, as this discovery is called, is true only when the gas is kept at a steady temperature. As we saw in the previous chapter, most things expand when they are heated and contract when they are cooled. The link between the volume of a gas and its temperature was investigated by a French scientist, Jacques Charles, in 1798. He found that if a gas occupies a certain volume at 0°C, its volume will increase or decrease by 1/273 of that figure for each degree by which the temperature rises or falls. In the same way that Boyle's Law only applies when the temperature is constant, Charles's Law is only true if the pressure is kept constant. According to Charles's Law, if we could cool a gas down to absolute zero, -273.15°C, it would have no volume at all. Therefore, absolute zero must be the lowest possible temperature.

If all of the gas inside a hollow container could be removed, the empty space left would be called a total vacuum. The pressure inside the container would be zero and, unless the container was very strong, the pressure of the air outside would force it to collapse inwards. The first person to attempt to create a vacuum was a German engineer, Otto von Guericke. In 1654 he joined together two large metal hemispheres and pumped as much air as possible from the hollow space between them. He then harnessed horses to each

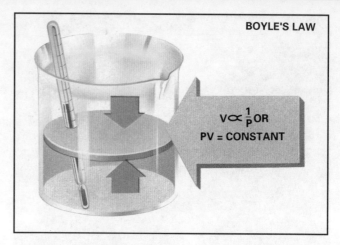

BOYLE'S LAW

$$V \propto \frac{1}{P} \text{ OR}$$
$$PV = \text{CONSTANT}$$

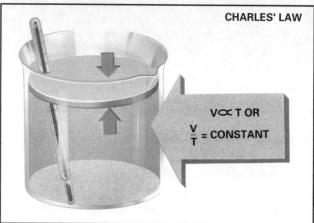

CHARLES' LAW

$$V \propto T \text{ OR}$$
$$\frac{V}{T} = \text{CONSTANT}$$

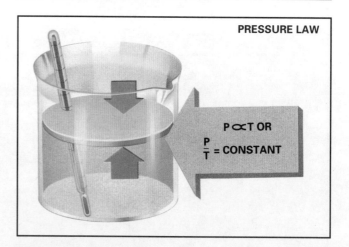

PRESSURE LAW

$$P \propto T \text{ OR}$$
$$\frac{P}{T} = \text{CONSTANT}$$

Above: The gas laws describe how gases behave in terms of pressure (P), volume (V) and temperature (T). $\propto$ means "is proportional to".

VON GUERICKE'S VACUUM EXPERIMENT 1654 • BOYLE'S LAW 1660 • CHARLES'S LAW 1798

hemisphere and made them pull in opposite directions. The two hemispheres only came apart when eight horses were pulling on each.

Liquid Gases

If a gas is cooled down enough, it will eventually turn to liquid. The temperature at which a gas does this is called its critical temperature. Most of the elements that exist naturally as gases, so-called permanent gases including oxygen, nitrogen and hydrogen, have very low critical temperatures and so they are very difficult to liquify. Before the invention of modern deep-freezing techniques, scientists were unable to cool gases to these low temperatures.

However, in 1818 the English scientist Michael Faraday discovered a way of liquefying gases by increasing the pressure as he cooled them. He successfully made liquefied hydrogen sulphide and sulphuric anhydride, but he could not produce enough pressure to liquefy other so-called permanent gases. Louis-Paul Cailletet finally succeeded with oxygen in 1877, Karl von Linde liquefied air in 1899 and James Dewar produced liquid hydrogen in the same year.

Below: The experiment carried out by Otto von Guericke in 1654 to demonstrate a vacuum.

HEAT TRANSFER

Heat can move from one place to another. There are three ways in which it does this: by conduction, convection and radiation. Both conduction and convection can only occur if there is matter present, because they involve moving molecules. Radiation, however, can travel through empty space.

Conduction and Convection

When a solid object is heated, the molecules close to the source of the heat start to vibrate more rapidly than when the object is cool. They collide with molecules near them and pass on some of their energy. These collisions continue and eventually the whole object becomes heated. The process by which heat spreads through solid objects is called conduction. Some materials, especially metals, are good conductors of heat. Materials that do not conduct heat well, such as rubber, wood and glass, are called insulators.

Gases and liquids (except mercury, which is a molten metal) are bad conductors of heat. Heat travels through them in a different way to convection. When a saucepan of cold water is heated, the water near the heat source expands and becomes less dense, which causes it to rise. Cold water sinks to the bottom to take its place and in turn is heated, expands and rises. Warm water at or near the surface cools down, becomes more dense, and sinks. The movement of the heated water sets up currents, called convection currents.

In the earth's atmosphere, huge convection currents cause winds to blow. When the sun warms the earth, the air above the land is heated. As the warm air rises, cooler air rushes in to take its place. Convection currents in the oceans transfer heat from the hot regions around the equator to cooler parts of the world. On a smaller scale, many people use convection to heat their homes. For example, in a central heating system the so-called radiators are actually convectors, which set up convection currents in the air to carry heat around the rooms of a house.

Radiation

A great deal of heat comes to us directly from the sun in the form of radiation. It reaches us after travelling 150 million km through empty space. Heat radiation was discovered in 1800 by an English astronomer, William Herschel. He noticed that when sunlight is passed

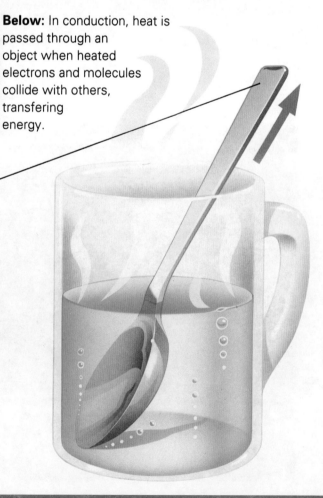

Below: In conduction, heat is passed through an object when heated electrons and molecules collide with others, transfering energy.

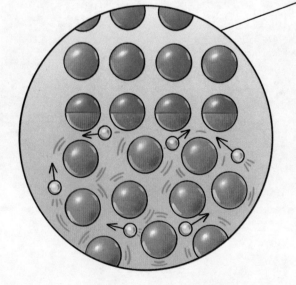

HEAT MOVES BY CONDUCTION, CONVECTION AND RADIATION

through a prism and split into its component colours, the red light gives off heat, which he detected with a thermometer. This happened because the light energy absorbed by the thermometer was converted into heat. Herschel also saw that the area just to one side of the beam of red light gave off heat. He concluded that the sun's rays carry energy other than light, and he named the rays of heat energy "infrared".

Infrared rays are similar to light rays, and they both travel at the same speed. They can be reflected, refracted (pp. 30-31) and absorbed. Shiny or light-coloured surfaces reflect heat better than dull or dark ones, and black objects absorb and radiate heat better than light-coloured ones.

Below: Convection currents in a heated saucepan of water. Hot water at the bottom rises, cools, sinks and is heated again.

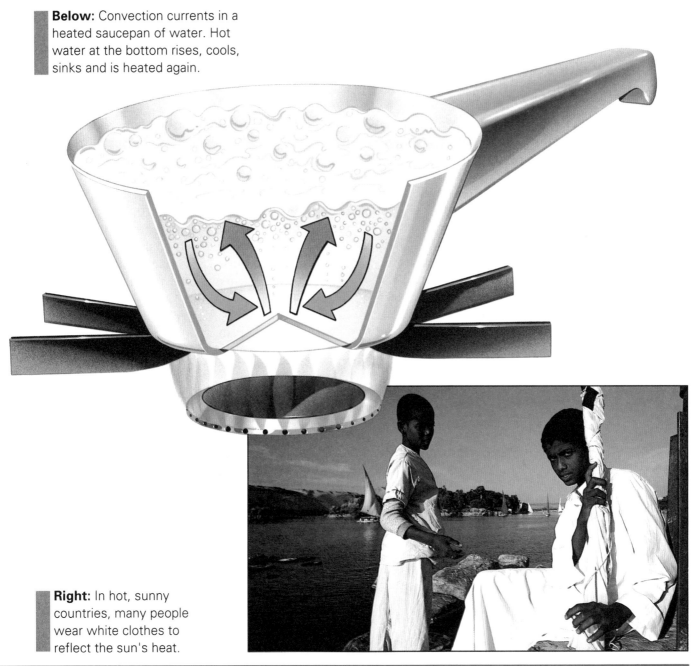

Right: In hot, sunny countries, many people wear white clothes to reflect the sun's heat.

LIGHT

The ancient Greeks thought that humans were able to see because their eyes gave out light that lit up objects in front of them, rather like the headlamps on a car. Like many of the Greeks' other scientific theories, this seemed to make common sense. However, it could not explain why things appear larger or smaller when they are moved towards or away from the eye.

A Cone of Rays

In about AD 1000 an Arab scientist, Alhazen, realized that we see an object because each part of it sends a ray of light into the eye. If you imagine looking at something round, like a saucer, the rays of light coming from its edges come together, or converge, as they get closer to the eye. The shape made by all the rays is like a cone, with its point at the eye. If the saucer is then moved closer to the eye, the cone of rays becomes shorter but wider, and so the saucer looks bigger. Despite the fact that Alhazen's idea was both simple and correct, it was ignored by most scientists for nearly 600 years.

Reflection, Refraction and Colour

People have known for thousands of years that light seems to travel in straight lines. Another early discovery was that when light hits a shiny surface it bounces off, or is reflected. When a ray of light strikes a flat mirror, the angle at which it reaches the mirror's surface (which is the angle of incidence) is the same as the angle at which it bounces off (the angle of reflection). If you look at something in a mirror, its image appears reversed left to right, and it also seems to be coming from behind the mirror.

When light rays pass into a transparent material, such as glass or water, they bend. This is called refraction. You can see it for yourself by putting a drinking straw into a glass of water. The light rays are refracted because glass and water are more dense than air, and the rays cannot travel through them as fast. When the rays enter the denser material they veer away from their normal path at an angle. They are refracted again when they emerge on the other side and pass back into the air.

Refraction is put to good use in lenses - pieces of glass or clear plastic with curved sides for spectacles, cameras, microscopes and other optical instruments. Lenses that bulge outwards are called convex lenses, and they bend light rays to make them converge at a point. The sides of a concave lens curve inwards, and they make light rays spread out.

A prism is a block of glass or clear plastic with ends that are triangular in shape. Since Aristotle's day, people have known that sunlight passing through a prism comes out in the form of a series of coloured rays. It was thought that the prism "stained" the light and made it coloured, but in 1666 Isaac Newton worked out what really happened inside the prism. He discovered that sunlight (so-called "white light") is actually made up of all the colours of the rainbow. When white light passes through a prism, the various colours are refracted at different angles and they spread out. Newton passed the coloured rays through a second prism and saw that they came together again as white light.

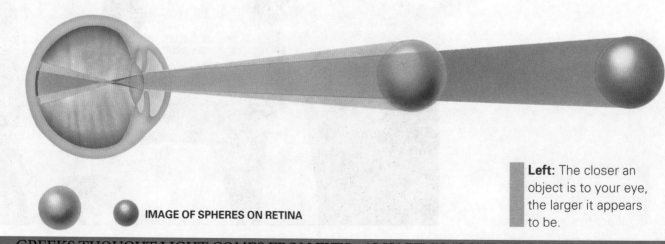

IMAGE OF SPHERES ON RETINA

Left: The closer an object is to your eye, the larger it appears to be.

GREEKS THOUGHT LIGHT COMES FROM EYES • ALHAZEN'S 'CONE OF RAYS' c. AD 1000

LENSES

A convex lens focuses light rays to a point. A concave lens spreads out the rays. Both lenses refract light rays passing through them.

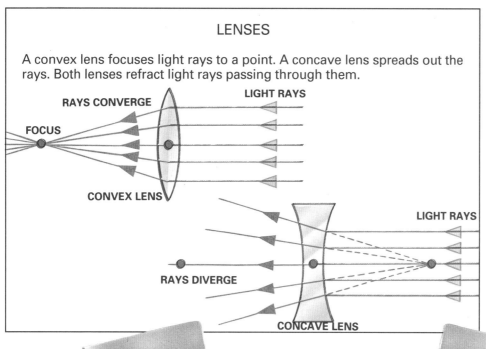

RAYS CONVERGE

LIGHT RAYS

FOCUS

CONVEX LENS

LIGHT RAYS

RAYS DIVERGE

CONCAVE LENS

Below: White light is refracted by these triangular glass prisms and split into its component colours.

NEWTON'S PRISM EXPERIMENTS PROVE WHITE LIGHT IS MIXTURE OF COLOURS 1666

NATURE OF LIGHT

As well as trying to discover how light behaves, scientists have attempted for hundreds of years to find out what light actually is. In the 1660s Isaac Newton thought light consisted of tiny particles, which he called corpuscles. A few years later Christiaan Huygens, a Dutch physicist, suggested that light travels in waves, rather like the ripples which spread out when you drop a stone into a pond.

Young and Light Waves

Even though Huygens's theory could explain why reflection and refraction occurred, not many people were convinced that light waves existed. The person who proved Huygens correct was an Englishman named Thomas Young.

In 1801, Young performed an experiment in which light shone on to a screen through two narrow slits which were side by side. The source of the light was a sodium lamp, which produced light of a pure colour.

When Young looked at the screen, he saw alternating light and dark bands. He noticed that they looked rather like the ripples in a pond when two stones are thrown in at the same time next to each other. The ripples, or waves, combine so that where two waves meet they make a wave of double height, and where two troughs meet they make a trough twice as deep. This is called wave interference. Young realized that the bands on the screen were an interference pattern, which meant that light must consist of waves.

Each wave has a peak and a trough, and the distance between each two wave peaks is called the wavelength. Light of one colour has a different wavelength from that of another colour. Young chose a sodium light source because he knew it gave light of a pure colour; that is, light of a single wavelength. When he repeated his experiment using white light, the bands on the screen became a complicated pattern of colours. The light had

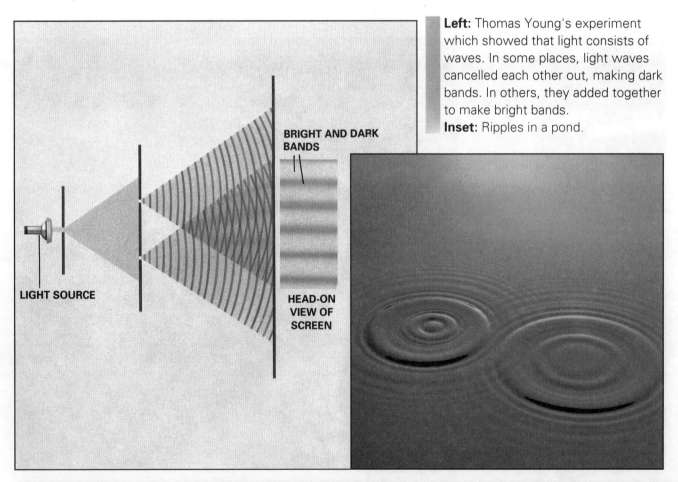

BRIGHT AND DARK BANDS

LIGHT SOURCE

HEAD-ON VIEW OF SCREEN

Left: Thomas Young's experiment which showed that light consists of waves. In some places, light waves cancelled each other out, making dark bands. In others, they added together to make bright bands.
Inset: Ripples in a pond.

NEWTON'S CORPUSCULAR THEORY OF LIGHT 1660s • YOUNG'S WAVE EXPERIMENTS 1801

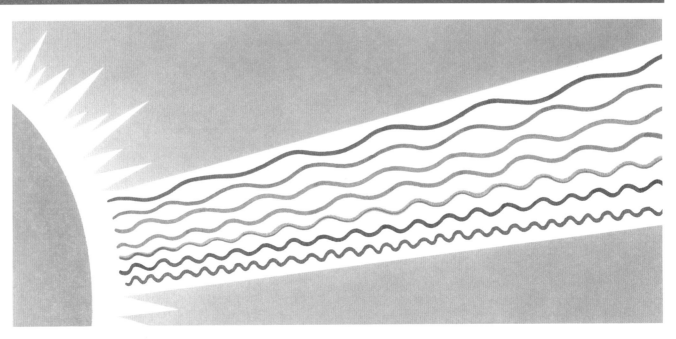

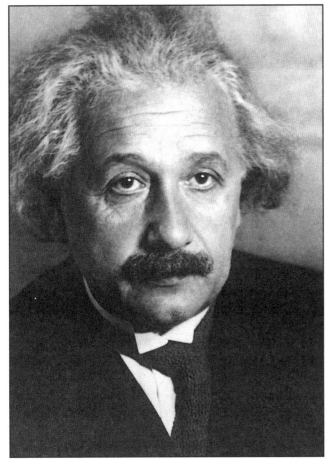

Left: Albert Einstein suggested that light is made of small packets of energy, called photons.

Above: White light consists of waves of coloured light with different wavelengths.

split into its different colours, making the interference pattern more difficult to interpret.

Einstein and Photons

In the early years of this century, the wave theory was modified by Albert Einstein. He suggested that light waves consist of small packets of energy, which were later named photons. In 1923 an American physicist called Compton found the first evidence that photons really do exist, and scientists today believe that light is made up of these particles travelling in waves. The way that light behaves depends upon certain circumstances. Sometimes it acts purely as a series of waves, but at other times the photons themselves seem more important and light will then behave as a stream of energy particles.

In his Theory of Relativity, Einstein predicted that nothing could travel faster than the speed of light. The first scientist to successfully measure the speed at which light travels in air was a Danish astronomer, Romer, who in 1676 calculated it to be 300,000 km per second.

EINSTEIN'S WAVES AND PHOTONS 1905 • COMPTON PROVES PHOTONS EXIST 1923

THE EYE

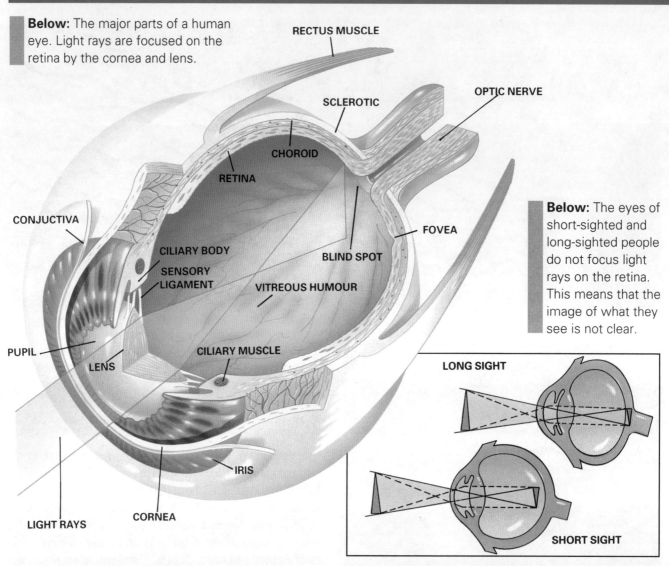

Below: The major parts of a human eye. Light rays are focused on the retina by the cornea and lens.

RECTUS MUSCLE

OPTIC NERVE

SCLEROTIC

CHOROID

RETINA

CONJUCTIVA

FOVEA

CILIARY BODY

SENSORY LIGAMENT

BLIND SPOT

VITREOUS HUMOUR

PUPIL

LENS

CILIARY MUSCLE

IRIS

LIGHT RAYS

CORNEA

Below: The eyes of short-sighted and long-sighted people do not focus light rays on the retina. This means that the image of what they see is not clear.

LONG SIGHT

SHORT SIGHT

We gather information about the world around us by using our five senses: sight, hearing, smell, taste and touch. Of these, sight is by far the most important, and 80 per cent of the information stored in the brain comes from the eyes.

The Human Eye

Light entering the eye is focused by the cornea, a transparent disc at the front of the eye and by the lens behind it. They refract the light rays and make them converge. Around the outside of the lens are tiny muscles which expand and contract in order to change its shape and make the image of what we are looking at sharper. In between the cornea and the lens is a coloured disc, the iris, with a hole in the middle, which is called the pupil. The pupil can be made larger to allow more light to enter the eye, or smaller to let through less light. In about 1850 the English surgeon Joseph Lister found that the iris was controlled by two separate sets of muscles, one set to make the pupil larger and the other to make it smaller.

When you look at something, the image of that object is focused on to the retina at the back of the eye, which consists of two types of minute cells, called rods and cones. Both are sensitive to light, although they work in different ways. Rods function in dim light and detect black and white, and cones only work in bright

Left: William Fox Talbot (1800-77). In 1841 he invented the calotype, the first process for making photographic negatives from which positives could be printed. He was also the first to use flash photography and his *Pencil of Nature* (1844) was the first book to be illustrated with photographs.

Left and below: A photographic positive, made from the negative (below) where the natural colours are reversed.

light and detect colour. This is why it is difficult to see colours clearly at night.

There is a small, highly sensitive area on the retina called the fovea, which contains only cones, closely packed together. When you look closely at an object the image falls on the fovea to help you see most clearly.

The image formed on the retina is upside down and has to be turned the correct way up inside the brain. Information about the image is sent from the eye to the brain along the optic nerve at the back of the eye. There are no light-sensitive cells at the point where the optic nerve joins the retina, and so we can't see the part of an image that falls on this so-called blind spot.

The brain receives information from each of our eyes and puts it together to form a single "picture". As our eyes are several centimetres apart they each receive a slightly different view of an object, and this gives us the ability to see in three dimensions.

Cameras

A camera works in a very similar way to the eye. It has a lens which focuses the image of an object, and an aperture like the pupil which can be made larger or smaller to let in more or less light. In modern cameras the image is formed on a piece of transparent plastic coated with light-sensitive chemicals, but earlier ones used metal or glass plates instead of plastic film.

The first photograph ever taken was by a French soldier, Nicéphore Niépce, in 1816. He had to wait a whole day for the image to form because the light-sensitive chemicals he used were very slow to work. Soon after, another Frenchman, Louis Daguerre, invented a much more sensitive, faster process, which meant that people could be photographed for the first time.

An important breakthrough was made by the Englishman William Fox Talbot. He found a simple way of producing first a "negative" image, in which black areas of an object appear white, and white parts are black, and then making any number of "positive" pictures from the negative.

ELECTROMAGNETIC WAVES

The light that we can see is known as the visible spectrum. At one end of this spectrum is red light, which has the longest wavelength that our eyes can detect, and at the other end is violet light, which has the shortest wavelength we can see.

Out of Sight

Beyond each end of the visible spectrum are waves with wavelengths that cannot be detected by our eyes. Waves just beyond those of violet light are called ultraviolet; although their shorter wavelength makes them invisible to us, the eyes of bees are sensitive to ultraviolet waves. On the far side of the red end of the visible spectrum are longer waves, which are called infrared. They too are outside our range of vision, although special "thermographic" cameras can take infrared pictures.

Infrared is also called thermal radiation. Thermal means "to do with heat", and this gives us a clue that light is not the only thing that travels in waves. Beyond infrared are microwaves and, with an even longer wavelength, radio waves. On the other side of the visible spectrum, with progressively shorter wavelengths, are X-rays and gamma rays.

Maxwell and Electromagnetic Waves

All of the waves just mentioned are parts of what is called the electromagnetic spectrum. The link between electricity and magnetism was first discovered in 1819 by a Danish scientist, Hans Christian Oersted. Some years later, the Scottish physicist James Clerk Maxwell proved mathematically that light waves were a combination of electricity and magnetism. He called such waves electromagnetic waves. However, he could not prove his theory experimentally.

In 1889 a German physicist, Heinrich Hertz, produced radio waves and was able to show that they, too, are electromagnetic waves which differ from light waves only in that they have longer wavelengths. Since then, scientists have discovered that X-rays, gamma rays, infrared and microwaves are also electromagnetic waves. They are all part of what is called the electromagnetic spectrum, and they all travel at the speed of light. The visible light that we can see falls roughly in the middle of the electromagnetic spectrum.

Modern science has found uses for all types of electromagnetic waves. Gamma rays and X-rays are

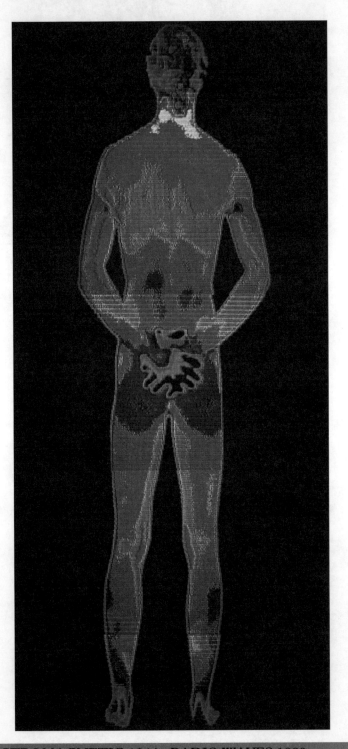

Below: A thermal image of a man. The hottest areas are white, and the coldest are dark blue or black.

Below: The electromagnetic spectrum. The wavelength increases from left to right, while the frequency decreases.

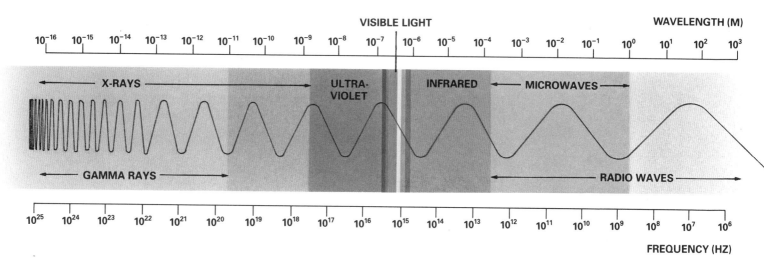

VISIBLE LIGHT

WAVELENGTH (M)

10^{-16} 10^{-15} 10^{-14} 10^{-13} 10^{-12} 10^{-11} 10^{-10} 10^{-9} 10^{-8} 10^{-7} 10^{-6} 10^{-5} 10^{-4} 10^{-3} 10^{-2} 10^{-1} 10^{0} 10^{1} 10^{2} 10^{3}

X-RAYS   ULTRA-VIOLET   INFRARED   MICROWAVES

GAMMA RAYS   RADIO WAVES

10^{25} 10^{24} 10^{23} 10^{22} 10^{21} 10^{20} 10^{19} 10^{18} 10^{17} 10^{16} 10^{15} 10^{14} 10^{13} 10^{12} 10^{11} 10^{10} 10^{9} 10^{8} 10^{7} 10^{6}

FREQUENCY (HZ)

used in medicine to kill cancer tumours in the body. They can be aimed very precisely at a tumour so that few healthy cells are damaged at the same time. X-rays are also used to take "pictures" of the body. They pass through the skin and tissues more easily than through bone, and so broken bones can be detected by placing the patient between an X-ray source and a metal screen that is sensitive to the rays. Microwaves can send telephone calls through the air and carry information to and from space satellites. They can also be used for cooking food. Radio waves are most commonly used to carry sound signals.

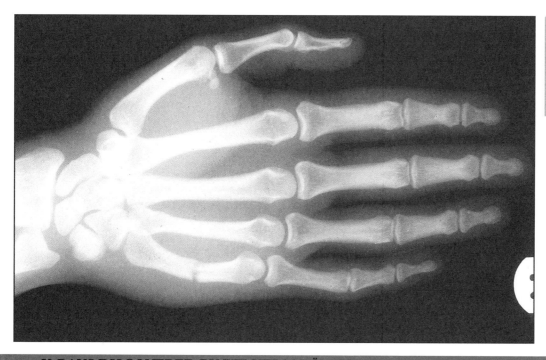

Left: An X-ray image of a human hand. The broken bone at the base of the little finger shows up clearly.

X-RAYS DISCOVERED BY WILHELM RÖNTGEN 1895 • FIRST MICROWAVE OVEN 1967

SOUND

There are quite a lot of similarities between sound and light. Both of them travel as waves, and can be reflected and refracted. However, they are produced in different ways and their waves are different, too.

Vibration and Sound Waves

Sounds are made when objects vibrate, or move quickly to and fro. If you pluck the string of a guitar or another stringed instrument you can see the string vibrate and hear the sound it makes. The sound of your voice is made by vocal chords inside your throat vibrating.

When an object vibrates it pushes the air molecules in front of it, bunching them up. The air molecules which are squashed together form a small area of high pressure. As the object moves back in the opposite direction, it leaves an area of low pressure where the air molecules are more spread out. These areas of high and low pressure move outwards from the vibrating object as sound waves.

This shows us that there is a very important differ-ence between light and sound. Light waves are electro-magnetic waves and they do not need air or any other "medium" to enable them to travel. Sound waves are vibration waves and they can only exist in a medium which has molecules that can be moved closer together and further apart. For example, as there is no air in outer space, there is no sound either; sometimes stars in far-away galaxies explode in complete silence.

Frequency, Amplitude and Speed

As in the case of light, the distance from the top of one sound wave to the next is called the wavelength. The number of complete sound waves or vibrations each second is called the frequency. The greater the fre-quency, the higher the pitch of the sound. Frequency is measured in hertz, named after Heinrich Hertz, the German physicist who experimented with radio waves in the late 1890s.

When the source of a sound is moving towards us it seems to have a higher pitch than when it is moving

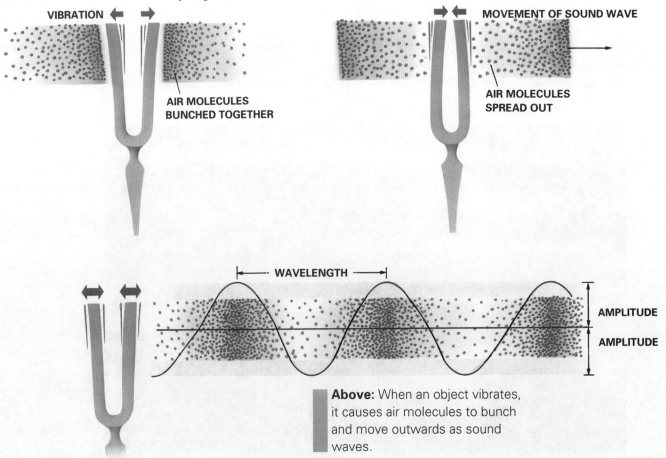

VIBRATION

AIR MOLECULES BUNCHED TOGETHER

MOVEMENT OF SOUND WAVE

AIR MOLECULES SPREAD OUT

WAVELENGTH

AMPLITUDE

AMPLITUDE

Above: When an object vibrates, it causes air molecules to bunch and move outwards as sound waves.

DOPPLER EFFECT OBSERVED BY CHRISTIAN DOPPLER 1845

38

away. This is called the Doppler effect, after Christian Doppler who discovered it in 1845. You can hear it for yourself if you listen to the siren of an ambulance or police car. It happens because the sound waves are squashed together as the siren approaches, making the frequency seem higher, and spread out more as the siren moves away.

The height of a sound wave is known as its amplitude. The larger the amplitude of a wave, the louder the sound. The loudness of sounds is measured in units called decibels.

The speed at which sound waves travel depends upon the medium through which they are moving. In air it is 332 metres per second, while in seawater it is nearly 1,500 metres per second. The speed of sound waves also increases as the temperature rises.

Sound waves can be reflected and refracted. They can also be diffracted, or bent around corners. Low-frequency sounds are diffracted more than higher ones.

Above: Part of Hertz's apparatus for studying waves.

Below: An example of the Doppler effect in action.

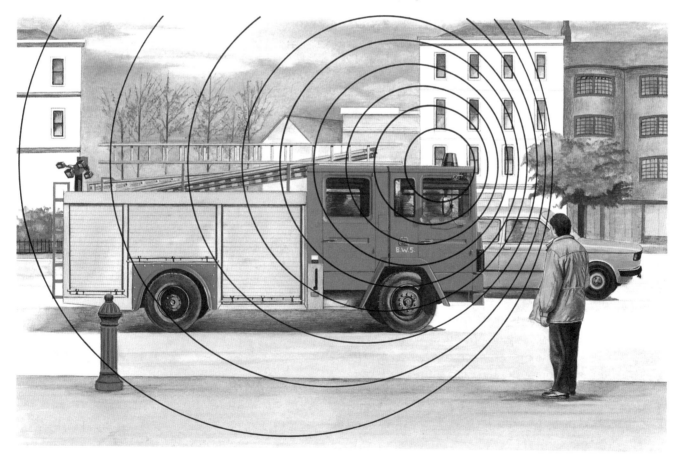

HEARING SOUND

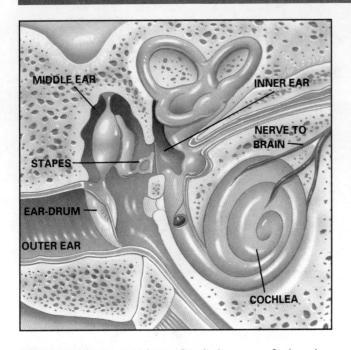

MIDDLE EAR
INNER EAR
NERVE TO BRAIN
STAPES
EAR-DRUM
OUTER EAR
COCHLEA

Humans, like many other animals, have ears for hearing sound. The flaps of skin on the sides of your head help to direct sound into a tube called the outer ear. At the end of this tube is the ear-drum, a thin, tightly stretched piece of skin which vibrates when sound waves reach it. The vibrations are passed on to the middle ear, which contains three small bones that act rather like levers and increase the force of the vibrations. The innermost bone, the stapes, pushes against another stretched piece of skin separating the middle ear from the inner ear. The inner ear is filled with fluid which is made to vibrate by the stapes, and the vibrations are picked up by thousands of sensitive hairs inside a coiled tube (the cochlea). The hairs then send signals to the brain which are interpreted as sounds.

What Can We Hear?

The softest sounds that human ears can detect are about as loud as the rustling of leaves. This sound has a loudness of just over 0 decibels. A normal conversation between two people is about 50 to 70 decibels, while the sound made by a jet aircraft is between 120 and 140 decibels. Sounds louder than 140 decibels can be painful and can damage our ears.

There are limits to the frequency of sound that our ears can hear. The lowest sound that most people can hear has a frequency of about 20 hertz. At the other end

of the scale, the highest sound adults can hear is about 16,000 hertz; young people have more sensitive ears and can hear frequencies up to about 20,000 hertz.

Ultrasound and Infrasound

Just as there are types of electromagnetic radiation that our eyes cannot see, there are also sounds that our ears are unable to hear. Sound waves with frequencies greater than 20,000 hertz are called ultrasound. Although we cannot hear ultrasound, many animals can. Dogs, for example, can hear up to about 35,000 hertz, while rats and mice squeak to each other at frequencies up to 100,000 hertz.

Some creatures rely much more on their ears than on their eyes. Insect-eating bats can detect a tiny insect in the dark at a distance of more than 20 m by sending out ultrasound clicks which bounce back from the intended prey as echoes. The bat's highly sensitive ears pick up the echoes, and the time between sending out

Above left: The main parts of the human ear that enable us to hear sounds.

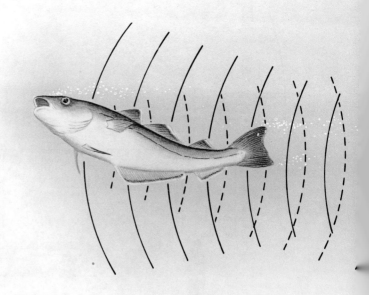

a click and hearing its echo tells the bat how far away the insect is. As it homes in on its prey, the bat speeds up its clicks to pinpoint the insect's position exactly.

Sound waves with frequencies lower than 20 hertz are known as infrasound. They can travel hundreds of kilometres. Tremors under the surface of the earth and waves at the seaside both produce infrasonic waves. Some very large creatures, such as elephants and whales, communicate with each other over long distances using infrasound.

Below: Dolphins use ultrasonic clicks to locate prey.

Right: An ultrasound image of a baby in its mother's womb.

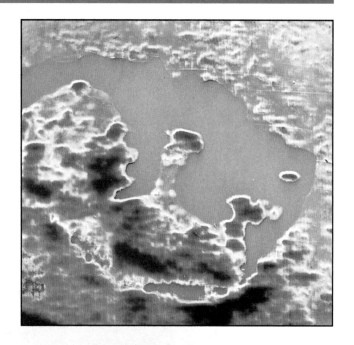

STATIC ELECTRICITY

Below: In 1752 Benjamin Franklin carried out an experiment in which he proved that lightning flashes are large electric sparks.

Above: The Leyden jar, invented in 1745, was the first device for storing electrical charges.

The ancient Greeks discovered electricity more than 2,500 years ago. In 600 BC a scientist called Thales noticed that amber, a natural resin, attracted silk fibres when they were being spun. The word electricity comes from the Greek name for amber, elektron.

Gilbert and du Fay

Very little progress was made in the study of electricity until William Gilbert, an Englishman, found that other materials besides amber could be electrified. It was Gilbert who first used the word electricity. Although he was successful with glass, he could not electrify metals and he believed that was impossible. In 1734 he was proved wrong by the French scientist Charles du Fay. He found that metals could be electrified, but only if they were held in a handle made of glass or amber and not in the hand.

In his experiments, du Fay discovered another important fact: there are two kinds of electrification, which were later called positive and negative charges. A positive charge and a negative charge attract one another, while two charges that are the same push each other away. You can demonstrate this by rubbing an inflated balloon on a woollen sweater, which gives the balloon a negative charge. If you hold it up to a wall it will stay there, because its negative charges are attracted to the positive charges in the wall. If you negatively charge two balloons and hold them together they will push apart because they both have the same charge.

Between 1727 and 1729, Stephen Gray had found that electricity could flow freely through certain things, such as the human body and water. Other materials, such as glass and amber, would not allow electricity to flow through them. The French inventor Jean Desaguliers called materials through which electricity flows easily "conductors", and those through which it would not "insulators".

Storing Charge

In 1745 a device was invented in which electrical charges could be stored. Such things are now called capacitors. The Leyden jar, made by Petrus van Musschenbroek, became an object of curiosity throughout Europe and people travelled from far and wide to see how it produced electricity.

This development led Benjamin Franklin, an American scientist and inventor, to carry out a famous, and very dangerous, experiment in 1752. He tied a key to the string of a kite and flew the kite during a lightning storm. Electricity flowed down the string and made a spark on the key. By using lightning to charge a Leyden jar, Franklin proved that it was a large electric spark that carried electricity from thunderclouds to the ground. He later made a fortune selling his lightning conductor, a metal strip that runs from the top of a tall building to the ground and carries away electricity safely if the building is struck by lightning.

In 1785 Charles de Coulomb, a French physicist, was able to describe the basic laws of static electricity (electricity that stays in one place and does not move). One of these was that the force of attraction or repulsion between two charged objects depends upon the distance between them. The unit in which electric charge is measured is now called the coulomb in his honour.

ELECTRIC CURRENTS

When electricity moves through a conductor, we say that an electric current is flowing. A current moves along a wire rather like water flows through a pipe. Like the water, a current needs a force to push it along the wire. This electrical force can be provided by a battery.

Volta's Chemical Battery

The first battery was invented in 1799 by the Italian scientist Alessandro Volta. He made it from layers of silver, blotting paper soaked in sulphuric acid, and zinc. Electrical force, or potential difference as it is often known, is now measured in units called volts.

The size of the current that flows through a wire depends to some extent on the potential difference. A larger potential difference will produce a larger current. Electric currents are measured in units called amperes, after André Marie Ampère, the Frenchman who car-

ried out early experiments on currents in the 1820s.

There is also another factor which affects the size of a current. Water slows down as it passes through a pipe (because of friction), and so does electric current flowing through a wire. The slowing down of a current is caused by resistance. It is measured in ohms, after Georg Simon Ohm who experimented with currents flowing through electric circuits. (The simplest electric circuit consists of a wire connected to a battery in an unbroken path.) In 1827 he discovered that the resistance of a wire equals the potential difference, or voltage, divided by the current. Known as Ohm's Law, this means that if a circuit has a high resistance, a large voltage is needed to make a current flow.

In 1841 James Prescott Joule, an English physicist, found that when a current flows through a wire, the wire

Below: A simple electric circuit consisting of a battery, wires and a bulb. The arrows show the direction in which current flows.

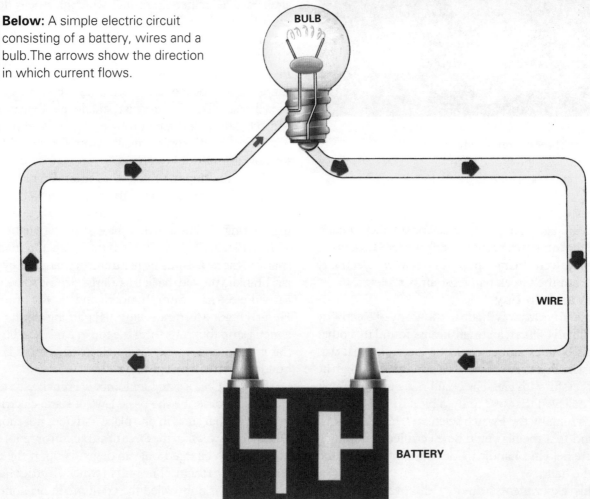

BULB

WIRE

BATTERY

heats up. This effect is caused by the resistance of the wire. The thinner the wire, the greater the resistance, and the greater the amount of heat produced. An electric light bulb contains very thin wire of high resistance which glows when it heats up. The fuse in an electric plug uses the Joule effect as a safety measure. It has a fixed resistance so that if too large a current flows through it the fuse melts (harmlessly inside an insulated casing) and breaks the circuit.

The type of current produced by a battery is called direct current, or DC. The electricity that we use in our homes, for such things as lights and electrical appliances like fridges and televisions, is of a different type, called alternating current, or AC. This type of current flows around a circuit first in one direction and then in the other.

The Origin of Electricity

By the mid-nineteenth century, scientists knew a great deal about how electricity behaves, but they did not know where it came from. In 1897 Joseph John Thomson discovered that atoms contain particles called electrons. Each electron has a tiny negative charge, and it is the movement of electrons that produces electricity.

When a balloon is rubbed on wool, it becomes negatively charged because electrons are transferred from the wool to the balloon. An electric current flowing along a wire is actually a stream of electrons moving from the negative terminal of a battery towards the positive terminal. Resistance occurs because the electrons sometimes collide with the metal atoms in the wire. These collisions produce the heat that Joule noticed in 1841.

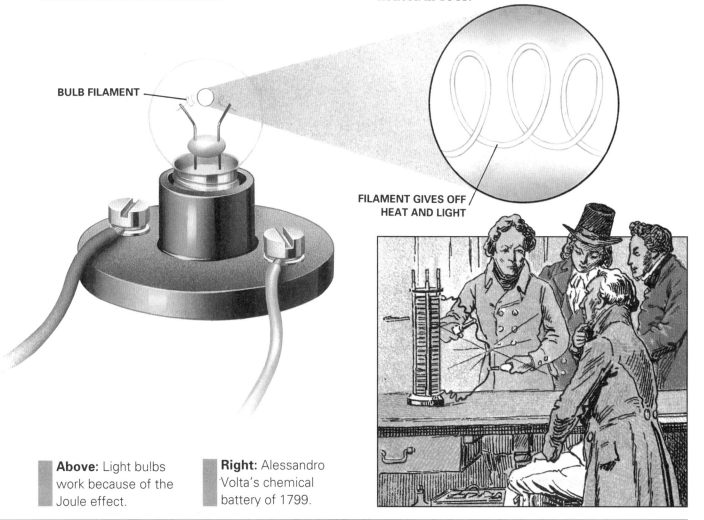

BULB FILAMENT

FILAMENT GIVES OFF
HEAT AND LIGHT

Above: Light bulbs work because of the Joule effect.

Right: Alessandro Volta's chemical battery of 1799.

MAGNETISM

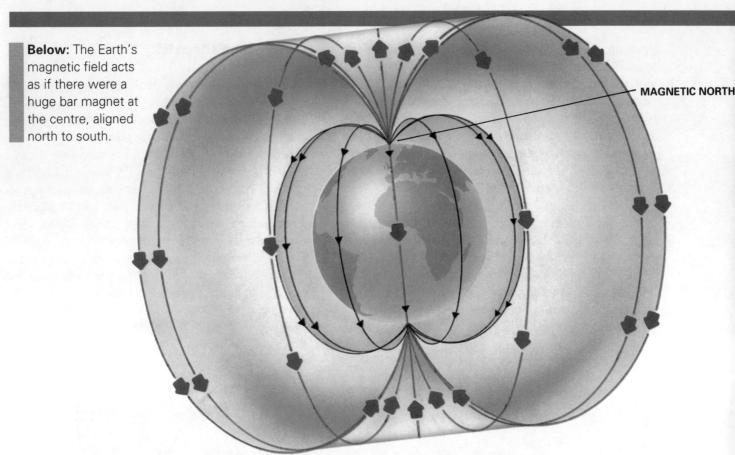

Below: The Earth's magnetic field acts as if there were a huge bar magnet at the centre, aligned north to south.

MAGNETIC NORTH

As is the case in many other areas of science, the ancient Greeks knew about magnetism 2,500 years ago. They discovered rocks which could pick up small pieces of iron, such as nails.

Magnets and Fields

Magnets attract objects made of iron, steel and some other metals. However, most metals, including copper, aluminium and gold, are non-magnetic, and so are cloth, paper, glass and plastic.

Not all parts of a magnet are equally magnetic; the strongest points are usually near to the ends of a magnet, and are called the north pole and south pole. In the thirteenth century a scientist called Peter Peregrinus found that the north pole of one magnet attracts the south pole of another, while two north poles (or two south poles) repel each other.

The area around a magnet in which magnetism can be detected is called a magnetic field. The field is strongest near the poles and gets weaker further away from them. In the sixteenth century the Englishman William Gilbert realized that the Earth itself is an enormous magnet, with a north and a south pole. These magnetic poles are not in the same place as the geographic North Pole and South Pole.

If a magnet is able to move freely, it will turn in order to line itself up with the Earth's field, so that one end, the north pole, points towards the north, and the south pole points south. A compass consists of a magnetic needle which points north and helps navigators in ships and aircraft to know the direction in which they are travelling. The Earth's magnetic field can also be detected 80,000 km into space.

You can magnetize a steel needle by stroking it with a magnet. This is possible because the atoms inside a magnetic material, like steel, are all tiny magnets themselves. When the needle is stroked with the magnet all of the atoms line up to point in the same direction, with their north poles facing one way and their south poles facing the other.

Electricity and Magnetism

In 1819 Hans Christian Oersted discovered that an electric current flowing through a wire moved the

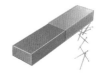

needle of a nearby compass. The current had produced a magnetic field around the wire. This phenomenon is known as electromagnetism. The strength of a field produced in this way depends upon the size of the current, the length of the wire and the distance from the wire.

The first electromagnet was made in 1820 by François Arago. He coiled copper wire around an iron bar and passed a current through it. The coil produced a magnetic field which magnetized the iron bar. The strength of an electromagnetic field increases if the current passed through the coil is made larger, and if the number of turns of wire in the coil is increased.

Following the work of Oersted, Arago and others, Michael Faraday tried to do the reverse of what they had achieved: produce an electric current using a magnetic field, known as electromagnetic induction. He struggled with the problem for 6 years, and finally succeeded in 1831. Faraday's achievement led to the development of generators, which produce electricity from the movement of a wire through a magnetic field. An electric motor works in the opposite way: an electric current flowing through a wire in a magnetic field causes the wire to move.

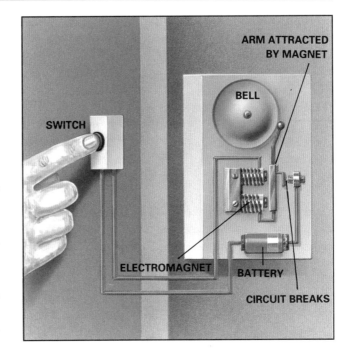

Above: An electric bell uses an electro-magnet.

Below: Michael Faraday at work in his laboratory.

ARAGO'S ELECTROMAGNET 1820 • FARADAY'S ELECTROMAGNETIC INDUCTION 1831

COMPUTERS

Computers are machines designed to store, recall and process information. The effectiveness or power of a computer is usually measured in terms of the amount of information it can store in its memory, and the number of instructions it can carry out per second.

The First Computers

The origins of the computer date back 5,000 years to the invention of the abacus. During the seventeenth century mechanical calculating machines were devised by Blaise Pascal, Gottfried von Liebnitz and others, but one of the most important advances came from an unlikely direction, silk weaving machines. In 1805 the Frenchman Joseph-Marie Jacquard invented a loom which could be programmed to weave different patterns by inserting one of a number of cards with holes punched in various positions. Thirty years later, Charles Babbage designed what he called the Analytical Engine, a calculating machine into which information was inserted by means of punched cards.

In 1886 Hermann Hollerich combined the advances made by Jacquard and Babbage with new electromagnetic inventions to produce a machine which could sort information into different categories. An American, George Stibitz, invented the first binary computer in 1939. Binary means "two", and in the binary system only two digits (1 and 0) are used to express numbers. In binary computers, the digit 1 means that an electric current flows and 0 means that no current flows. All modern computers use the binary system.

The world's first successful computer, called ENIAC (Electronic Numerical Integrator and Calculator), was built in 1946. It contained over 18,000 switches called valves, and filled a large room. Two years later came UNIVAC (Universal Automatic Computer), the first machine to be programmed with information on magnetic tape instead of punched tape or cards.

Semiconductors and Silicon Chips

When you think of a modern computer, you probably think of a small machine that fits quite neatly on top of a desk. Despite its size, a desktop computer may contain hundreds of thousands of electronic parts. How do they all fit inside?

Until fairly recently, the electronic components from which computers were made were all quite large

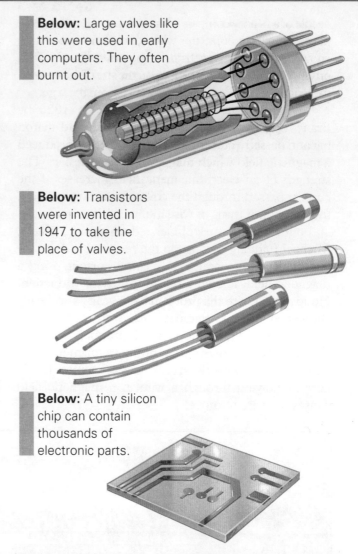

Below: Large valves like this were used in early computers. They often burnt out.

Below: Transistors were invented in 1947 to take the place of valves.

Below: A tiny silicon chip can contain thousands of electronic parts.

and bulky. The first step towards building smaller computers came with the use of materials known as semiconductors. Normally, semiconductors do not conduct electricity, but under certain conditions they allow a very small electric current to flow. In 1947 William Shockley, John Bardeen and Walter Brattain found a way of using semiconductors to make a new type of switch, the transistor. Transistors are only a fraction of the size of valves, and their invention revolutionized computers. Even so, computers of the 1950s were much larger and less powerful than those of today.

Then, in 1958, an American company, Texas Instruments, developed the integrated circuit. This consisted of a thin slice of silicon (a semiconductor) on

Above: ENIAC, the first electronic computer, and a modern personal computer. Despite its size, the modern one is far more powerful.

Below: A magnified view of a modern silicon chip, showing the vast number of electronic components it contains.

which were placed a variety of electronic components, including transistors, all connected with tiny threads of metal. Integrated circuits soon became known as silicon chips, microchips or, simply, chips.

Since then, it has become possible to put more and more components on a chip. Several thousand components can now be fitted on to a chip no bigger than a fingernail. In 1990 one manufacturer produced a chip, 14 cm square, with 4 million transistors crammed on to its surface.

The largest modern computers, called supercomputers, are staggeringly powerful. One of these, the Cray-2, contains over 200,000 silicon chips and can carry out several billion calculations every second.

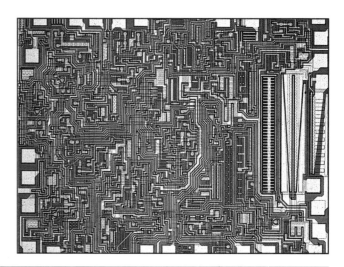

ENIAC COMPUTER 1946 • TRANSISTOR INVENTED 1947 • FIRST INTEGRATED CIRCUIT 1958

RADIOACTIVITY

Not all scientific discoveries are made as a result of scientists working to solve a particular problem; some happen by pure chance. One of the most famous "accidental" discoveries was that of radioactivity.

Becquerel and the Curies

One day in 1896, the Frenchman Henri Becquerel began an experiment. He wanted to see if a substance containing uranium gave off X-rays (which had been discovered the previous year) when exposed to sunlight. He could not finish the experiment because the weather was too cloudy, and he put away his equipment. A few days later he tried again, and placed the uranium samples on a photographic plate that had not been taken out of its wrapping. Later, when he developed the plate, he was surprised to see an image that matched the shapes of the samples. He concluded that the uranium was giving off rays, which he called radiation, that affected the photographic plate but he did not understand how the radiation was produced.

Becquerel took the problem to his friends, Pierre and Marie Curie. They spent 2 years examining pitchblende (the ore from which uranium comes) and, in 1898, found that it contained two previously unknown elements, which were given the names radium and polonium. Both of these elements gave off radiation much more strongly than uranium.

In 1899 Ernest Rutherford found that uranium gave off two types of radiation, which he call alpha and beta rays. A third type, gamma rays, was discovered in 1900. Two years later the English physicist Frederick Soddy was able to explain how radioactivity was produced. He showed that the nuclei of some atoms are unstable and, as a result, they break up and give off energy in the form of radiation.

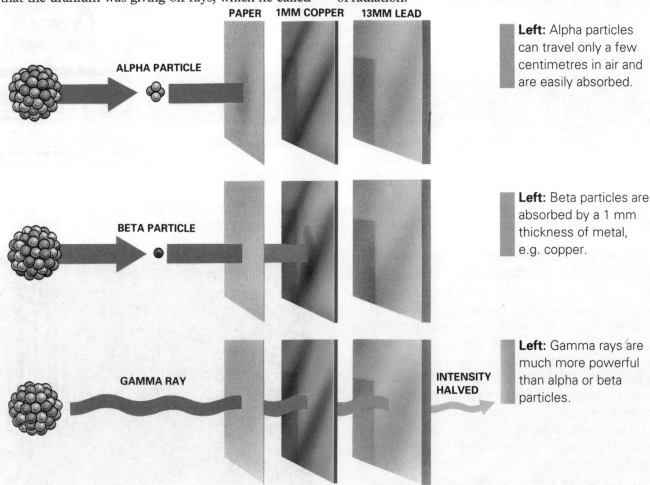

PAPER **1MM COPPER** **13MM LEAD**

ALPHA PARTICLE

Left: Alpha particles can travel only a few centimetres in air and are easily absorbed.

BETA PARTICLE

Left: Beta particles are absorbed by a 1 mm thickness of metal, e.g. copper.

GAMMA RAY **INTENSITY HALVED**

Left: Gamma rays are much more powerful than alpha or beta particles.

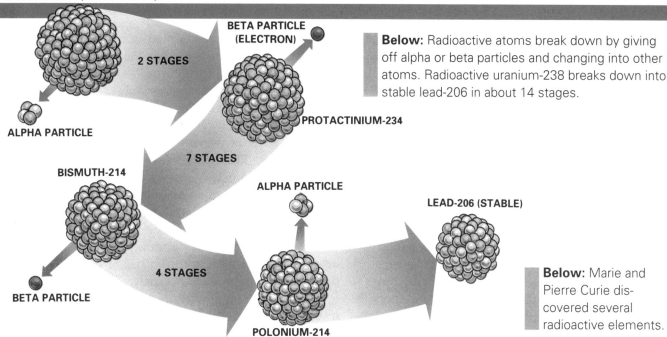

URANIUM-238 (RADIOACTIVE)

BETA PARTICLE
(ELECTRON)

2 STAGES

ALPHA PARTICLE

PROTACTINIUM-234

7 STAGES

BISMUTH-214

ALPHA PARTICLE

LEAD-206 (STABLE)

4 STAGES

BETA PARTICLE

POLONIUM-214

Below: Radioactive atoms break down by giving off alpha or beta particles and changing into other atoms. Radioactive uranium-238 breaks down into stable lead-206 in about 14 stages.

Below: Marie and Pierre Curie discovered several radioactive elements.

The atoms of a particular element all have the same number of protons in their nuclei, but some may have more neutrons than others. Atoms of one element which have different numbers of neutrons are called isotopes, and almost all elements have several such isotopes. Many isotopes are quite stable and do not change. Others are unstable and as their nuclei break up, or decay, they give off radiation. (This is just as Soddy suggested, although he did not know what caused instability in the nucleus as neutrons were not discovered until 1932.)

In 1934 the Curie family made another breakthrough. All of the work on radioactivity had been carried out using radioactive elements that occur naturally. Irène and Frédéric Joliot-Curie (daughter and son-in-law of Pierre and Marie) made an "artificially" radioactive isotope by bombarding aluminium with alpha particles. Their success has led to the production of many other new radioactive isotopes which are used in biology, medicine and other scientific fields.

Half-life and Radiocarbon Dating

Different radioactive isotopes break down at different rates. The speed at which they break down is measured in terms of what is called half-life. This is the time it takes for half of the nuclei in a radioactive sample to decay. Some isotopes have half-lives of a fraction of a second, while others are much longer.

An isotope of carbon, called carbon-14, has a half-life of 5,730 years. As carbon is one of the most common elements found on earth, the decay of its radioactive isotope has given us a method of telling how old some materials are. By measuring the amount of carbon-14 still present in the material, and knowing the half-life, scientists can calculate its age.

FISSION AND FUSION

The nucleus at the centre of an atom contains huge amounts of energy. This energy can be released in what are called nuclear reactions.

Nuclear Fission

Fission is a nuclear reaction in which a heavy, unstable nucleus is split into two or more lighter nuclei. In the process, a number of neutrons are given off.

Sometimes fission occurs naturally, but in the main it is made to happen by artificial methods. Not all nuclei can be made to fission; those which can, such as the isotopes plutonium-239 and uranium-235, are described as being fissile.

The most common method of producing fission is to fire a particle, such as a neutron, at a heavy nucleus. When the nucleus absorbs the neutron it becomes unstable and fissions. It gives out neutrons and energy in the form of heat. If there are other heavy nuclei present, they may be hit by the neutrons, causing more fissions, and so on. This is called a chain reaction. The minimum amount of material which needs to be present for a chain reaction to happen is known as the critical mass. The first so-called atomic pile in which fission was produced was made in the USA in 1942, by the Italian scientist Enrico Fermi.

Nuclear fission is most commonly used in nuclear power stations. The fuel used in the reactors of most nuclear power stations is in the form of rods containing uranium, some of which is uranium-235 and some uranium-238. The most reactive of these is uranium-235. When its nucleus absorbs a neutron, it breaks down into isotopes of lanthanum and bromine, and gives off three neutrons and some heat. The chain reaction that takes place inside the reactor can be controlled by inserting or withdrawing fuel rods. The heat produced is used to turn water to steam, which turns turbines to produce electricity.

The first nuclear power station to produce electricity was built in the USA in 1951. A major drawback to the use of nuclear power stations is that the isotopes produced during fission are highly radioactive, and dangerous to living things.

The other use of fission is much more dangerous:

Below: In nuclear fission, a nucleus absorbs a neutron fired at it, becomes unstable, and breaks down to give off energy as heat.

Below: In nuclear fusion, two light nuclei are forced to combine into a single heavy one. Large amounts of energy are released.

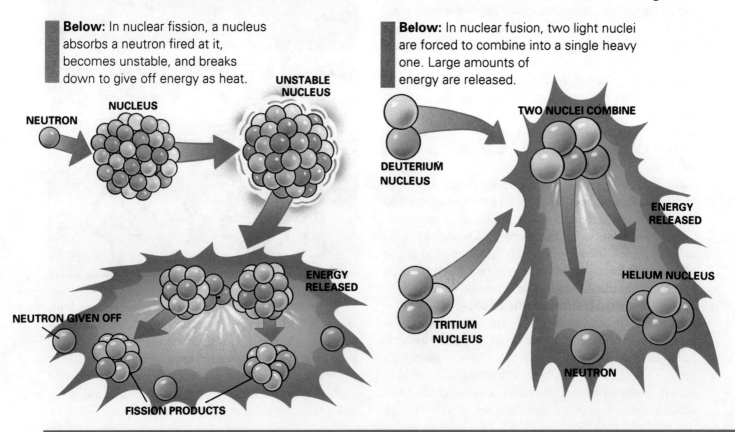

NEUTRON

NUCLEUS

UNSTABLE NUCLEUS

ENERGY RELEASED

NEUTRON GIVEN OFF

FISSION PRODUCTS

DEUTERIUM NUCLEUS

TWO NUCLEI COMBINE

ENERGY RELEASED

HELIUM NUCLEUS

TRITIUM NUCLEUS

NEUTRON

nuclear weapons. Although the fission process is the same inside both a reactor and a nuclear bomb, the chain reaction in a bomb is not controlled and so it causes an explosion and a massive release of energy.

Nuclear Fusion

Fusion occurs in a different way from fission. Instead of heavy nuclei breaking down into lighter ones, two light nuclei are made to collide and join together to make a single heavy one. An example of a fusion reaction is that between deuterium and tritium (two isotopes of hydrogen) which, on collision, produce helium, a single neutron and energy.

Nuclear fusion can only occur at extremely high temperatures, measured in millions of degrees Celsius. For this reason, fusion happens naturally only inside the sun and other stars. Uncontrolled fusion reactions have been carried out in the form of hydrogen bombs, but fusion cannot yet be put to more peaceful purposes. Scientists are trying to devise ways of building a fusion reactor. However, the problems of containing fuel at such high temperatures are, at present, impossible to solve. If the scientists succeed, the world's energy problems could be solved. What is more, unlike fission, fusion does not produce radioactive waste.

Below: A nuclear bomb is an example of an uncontrolled fission reaction. Huge amounts of energy are released by the explosion.

FIRST NUCLEAR POWER STATION BUILT 1951 • HYDROGEN BOMB DEVELOPED, USA 1952

CHEMISTRY

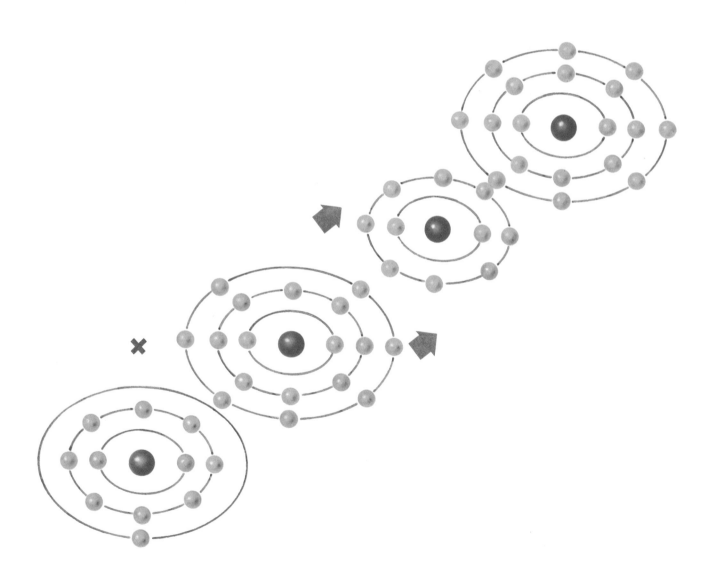

ELEMENTS

Everything in the Universe consists of combinations of substances called elements. The ancient Greeks believed that things on Earth were made of just four elements, earth, air, fire and water, while the rest of the Universe consisted of a fifth element, ether.

Scientists have discovered that in fact there are 92 elements which occur naturally on Earth, and they are not at all like those of the Greeks. Of these 92 "native" elements, only two, bromine and mercury, are liquids at normal temperature, 11 are gases and the rest are all solids. Most of the solids are metals.

One of the first elements to be identified was gold. This is because it appears in pure lumps, called nuggets. Many other elements do not occur in such a convenient form, but in combinations of elements known as compounds (pp. 58-59). Most such elements have been found by breaking down compounds. Silicon, which occus in sand and other substances, is the second most common element on Earth after oxygen. It was first made in its pure form in 1823 by Jöns Jakob

Berzelius. Aluminium occurs in an ore called bauxite, in which it is combined with oxygen. The Danish scientist Hans Christian Oersted succeeded in separating out aluminium in 1825.

In recent years, scientists have made 18 new elements artificially, taking the total number up to 110. All of the new elements are radioactive, and most have been created using particle accelerators. Experiments are now underway to make the 111th element.

Elements and Atoms

We now know that an element is a substance which is made up of just one kind of atom. The element iron, for example, contains only iron atoms, which are different from the atoms of all other elements. This means that elements cannot be broken down into other, simpler substances.

What makes an atom of one element different from that of another is the number of protons inside the nucleus. This is called the atomic number. Hydrogen has a single proton, so its atomic number is 1; iron has

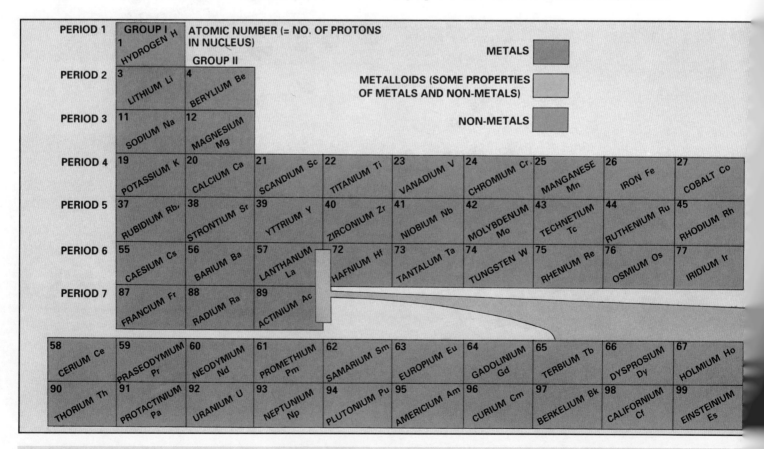

MATTER MADE OF 92 ELEMENTS & THEIR COMPOUNDS WITH 18 MAN-MADE ELEMENTS

26 protons and an atomic number of 26.

The Periodic Table

One of the most important developments in modern science was the drawing up of the Periodic Table of Elements. This was the work of a Russian scientist, Dmitri Mendeleev, in 1869. The illustration on this page shows a modern version of the table. Elements are arranged according to their atomic number, and each has a chemical symbol; the symbol for hydrogen is H, while that of gold is Au.

The vertical columns, or "groups", contain elements that have similar properties. The group on the right-hand side, for example, contains helium, neon, argon, krypton, xenon and radon, all of which are gases that do not combine, or "react", easily with other elements to form compounds. As you move to the left along a horizontal row, or "period", the elements become steadily more reactive, and those in the left-hand group are the most reactive of all. How reactive an element is depends on the way in which the electrons are arranged in its atoms.

Below: A modern version of the Periodic Table.

Right: New elements can be made using particle accelerators.

			GROUP III	GROUP IV	GROUP V	GROUP VI	GROUP VII	GROUP VIII
								2 HELIUM He
			5 BORON B	6 CARBON C	7 NITROGEN N	8 OXYGEN O	9 FLUORINE F	10 NEON Ne
			13 ALUMINIUM Al	14 SILICON Si	15 PHOSPHORUS P	16 SULPHUR S	17 CHLORINE Cl	18 ARGON Ar
28 NICKEL Ni	29 COPPER Cu	30 ZINC Zn	31 GALLIUM Ga	32 GERMANIUM Ge	33 ARSENIC As	34 SELENIUM Se	35 BROMINE Br	36 KRYPTON Kr
46 PALLADIUM Pd	47 SILVER Ag	48 CADMIUM Cd	49 INDIUM In	50 TIN Sn	51 ANTIMONY Sb	52 TELLURIUM Te	53 IODINE I	54 XENON Xe
78 PLATINUM Pt	79 GOLD Au	80 MERCURY Hg	81 THALLIUM Tl	82 LEAD Pb	83 BISMUTH Bi	84 POLONIUM Po	85 ASTATINE At	86 RADON Rn

68 ERBIUM Er	69 THULIUM Tm	70 YTTERBIUM Yb	71 LUTETIUM Lu					
100 FERMIUM Fm	101 MENDELEVIUM Md	102 NOBELIUM No	103 LAWRENCIUM Lw	104 UNNILQUADIUM Unq	105 UNNILPENTIUM Unp	106 UNNILHEXIUM Unh	107 UNNILSEPTIUM Uns	108 UNNILOCTIUM Uno	109 UNNILENNIUM Une

MENDELEEV'S PERIODIC TABLE 1869 • ELEMENT REACTION DEPENDS ON ELECTRONS

COMPOUNDS

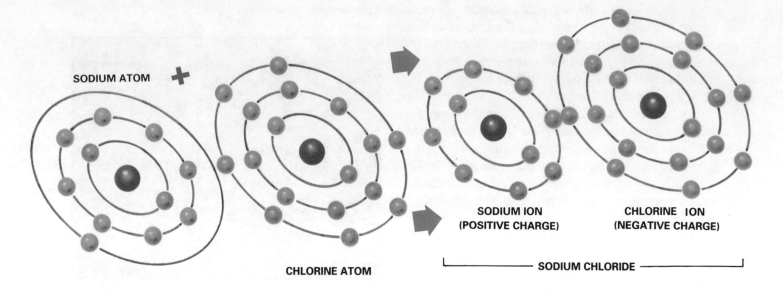

SODIUM ATOM

CHLORINE ATOM

SODIUM ION
(POSITIVE CHARGE)

CHLORINE ION
(NEGATIVE CHARGE)

SODIUM CHLORIDE

Some chemical elements are more likely than others to react and form compounds. As we have seen, those in the left-hand group of the Periodic Table are the most reactive elements, while those in the right-hand group rarely react at all. The reactiveness of an element totally depends upon the location of the electrons inside its atoms.

Chemical Bonds

The electrons in an atom move around the central nucleus. Scientists think of them as occupying "shells", rather like the layers of an onion. Each shell can hold up to a certain number of electrons; the innermost shell, for example, can hold 2, and the next shell can have up to 8. Atoms are most stable when their shells are full. Neon, in the right-hand group, has 10 electrons which fill the first and second shells. It is very difficult to remove electrons from full shells.

The most reactive elements are those whose outer-most shell contains only a single electron. Sodium, for example, has a total of 11 electrons, 2 in the innermost shell, 8 in the second and 1 in the third. This lone

electron can easily be removed from the atom, which means that sodium is highly reactive. The elements in the last-but-one group on the right of the table have outer shells that are one electron short. Chlorine, for instance, has only 7 electrons in its outer shell, which means it can easily take in another electron. Not surprisingly, sodium and chlorine atoms react strongly with each other to form a compound called sodium chloride, or common salt.

When an atom gains or loses an electron it becomes electrically charged. Electrons each carry a negative charge while protons have a positive charge, so having an extra electron creates a negatively charged atom and losing an electron creates a positively charged atom. Thus, when sodium loses an electron it gains a positive charge which is attracted to the negatively charged chlorine. Atoms that carry an electrical charge are called ions, and the attraction between oppositely charged ions is called an ionic bond.

Not all of the bonds that hold atoms or molecules together are ionic. Sometimes pairs of electrons can be

IONIC BONDS HAVE TRANSFER OF ELECTRONS • COVALENT BONDS SHARE ELECTRONS

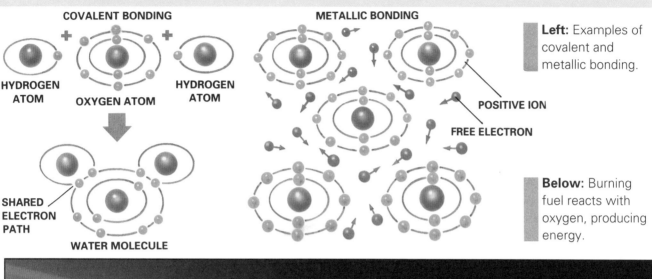

COVALENT BONDING

HYDROGEN ATOM

OXYGEN ATOM

HYDROGEN ATOM

SHARED ELECTRON PATH

WATER MOLECULE

METALLIC BONDING

POSITIVE ION

FREE ELECTRON

Left: Examples of covalent and metallic bonding.

Below: Burning fuel reacts with oxygen, producing energy.

shared between two atoms in what are called covalent bonds. Two chlorine atoms can share a pair of electrons, one from each, in order to fill their outer shells and make a stable chlorine molecule. A water molecule consists of a single oxygen atom sharing electrons with two hydrogen atoms.

The third type of chemical bonding is called metallic bonding. In a metal crystal, atoms lose some of their electrons and become positively charged ions. The lost electrons do not attach themselves to other atoms, but move around freely, rather like a "sea" of electrons that holds the metal ions together. These free-moving electrons help to explain why metals are good at conducting electricity and heat.

Reactions and Energy

When elements and compounds react to form new compounds, some molecules may be broken up and new ones created. These processes involve energy. Some reactions cannot start until extra energy is supplied in the form of heat. When coal (which is mainly carbon) burns it combines with oxygen in the air to form carbon dioxide. But coal will not start to burn unless it is heated. Other reactions may happen spontaneously and give off a great deal of energy. Sodium, for example, reacts very violently with water, giving off heat.

METALLIC BONDS HAVE "SEA" OF ELECTRONS • REACTIONS INVOLVE ENERGY CHANGES

THE
SCIENCE
OF LIFE

EVOLUTION

The Earth was formed around 4,600 million years ago, and the first life forms appeared some time before 3,200 million years ago. Since that time, life on Earth has developed from the first primitive plants and animals into the huge variety of life forms that now inhabit our planet. How did this happen?

The Fossil Record

Until early in the nineteenth century, it was widely believed that all life on the planet had been created at the same time. This idea came from the story of the creation in the Bible, and some religious scholars had even calculated a precise date on which it happened, 4004 BC.

However, this theory was being challenged by evidence in the form of fossils. A fossil is the name given to any physical evidence of life that existed long ago. Most fossils are found in rocks, and they formed when plants or animals, for example, became buried in mud soon after their death and gradually turned to stone. As well as plants and animals, fossil footprints have been found, and even ripple marks that were made by water in the mud beneath ancient seas.

Around 200 years ago, people began discovering fossils of creatures that no longer existed. The first dinosaur fossils, for example, were found in England in 1822. These finds led scientists to question the story of the creation.

Darwin and Evolution

In 1859 the English scientist Charles Darwin published a book called *On the Origin of Species by Means of Natural Selection*. The theory behind it was that the life we now see on Earth is the result of many millions of years of development, or evolution. The idea of evolution was not new; a Frenchman, Jean-Baptiste de Lamarck, had suggested in 1806 that creatures evolved in order to improve themselves. Nonetheless, Darwin's book shook the scientific world to its foundations.

The basis of Darwin's theory is that living things evolve because of two factors: adaptation and natural selection. In a species with many millions of individual plants or animals, there are always some with characteristics or types of behaviour that are slightly different from the rest. Most of these differences are of no use, but some may give individuals in a particular environ-

Below: The Galapagos Islands, and some of the unique species Charles Darwin found there.

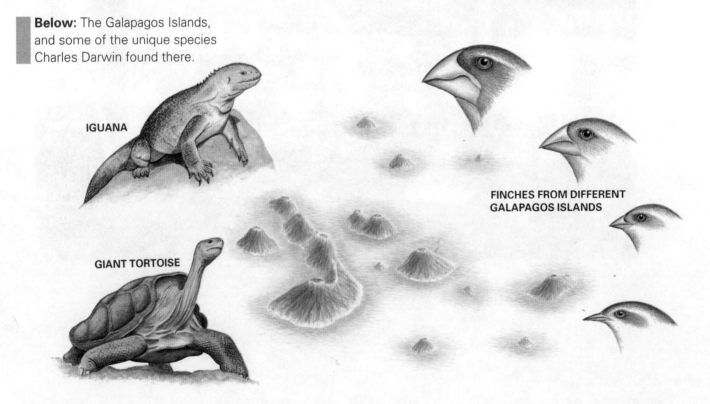

IGUANA

GIANT TORTOISE

FINCHES FROM DIFFERENT GALAPAGOS ISLANDS

LAMARCK'S THEORY OF EVOLUTION 1806 • FIRST DINOSAUR FOSSIL IN ENGLAND 1822

Above: The fossil of a Pterodactyl dinosaur.

Below: Some extinct plants and animals.

ment an advantage over the rest of the species. These beneficial changes are called adaptations. Over countless generations an adaptation may spread throughout a species in a particular area. The result of this is that a new species is created, different from the one still living in other areas where the adaptations were not useful because they did not suit the environment there.

Since life began, countless new species have appeared on Earth, and countless more have disappeared, or become extinct. According to Darwin, the survival or extinction of a species is decided by natural selection, or the survival of the fittest. When a particular type of food is in short supply and there are a number of different species that depend upon it, some individuals may be better adapted to the job of obtaining food. For example, animals with a long neck are able to reach leaves several metres above the ground when all the food lower down has been eaten. This enables them to survive when creatures with short necks die out. Over many generations, the adaptation that produced a long neck spreads through the species, passing from parents to offspring.

WOOLLY MAMMOTH

ARCHAEOPTERYX

ORTHOCERAS

GLOSSOPTERIS

TRILOBITE

RHYNIA

ORIGIN OF SPECIES 1859 • EVOLUTION THROUGH ADAPTATION & NATURAL SELECTION

MEDICAL DISCOVERIES

Below: The microscope was one of the most important inventions in medical science. This early example of a compound microscope was made c.1680.

Of all the creatures that have inhabited the earth since life first began, humans are the only ones which are able to think about and try to improve their lives. This is especially true where illnesses and their cures are concerned.

Medicine is as old as human civilization itself, but the ancient Greeks were among the first people to look closely at the human body and its workings, and to write down what they discovered. Much of their knowledge was passed on to later civilizations, including the Romans, and one of the first great physicians was a Roman by the name of Galen.

Born in AD 130, Galen became the surgeon of Emperor Marcus Aurelius. Like the Greeks before him, he believed that the four basic elements of earth, air, fire and water were absorbed into the body as food and drink, and that they caused certain characteristics, or "humours" in human behaviour. Galen constructed a complicated theory to explain how the organs and tubes of the body worked. It involved what he called Natural Spirits which existed in the liver and turned food into blood, and Vital Spirits that enriched the blood when it reached the heart.

The Dawn of Modern Medicine

Despite his close observation of the human body, Galen failed to realize that blood is pumped around it by the heart. This fact was discovered by an Englishman, William Harvey, in 1628. He observed that the heart consists of muscles which expand and contract, allowing blood to enter and then forcing it out again.

In 1665 another important discovery was made. Looking through a microscope at a piece of cork (which is dead plant tissue), Robert Hooke saw tiny structures which he called cells. At about the same time the Dutchman Anton van Leeuwenhoek identified cells in blood. Eventually, in 1824, the French scientist René Dutrochet established that the tissue of all living things consists of cells.

Tools and Techniques

As in other areas of science, advances in medicine happened partly because new techniques and equipment were developed. The first thermometer for medical use was invented in 1626 by an Italian physician, Santorio. In 1761 an Austrian called Auenbrügger invented the technique of percussion. This allowed doctors to detect the state of certain organs inside the body by tapping them with their fingers and listening to the sound. Sounds made by the body could be heard more accurately thanks to the invention of the stethoscope by René Laënnec in 1815. Four years later Jean-Louis Poiseuille invented the first manometer for measuring blood pressure.

Surgical operations were made much more bearable for patients by the invention of anaesthetics. Until the use of a gas called ether by C. W. Long in 1842, major surgery was agonisingly painful. Ether was later replaced by chloroform, which was first used by James Simpson in 1847.

One of the most important breakthroughs occurred even before those above, the invention of the microscope. No one is certain who invented it, but the first one was possibly made around 1600 by a Dutchman, Hans Jansen. In the 1660s Anton van Leeuwenhoek began grinding more accurate, powerful lenses which could magnify up to 300 times. As the science of making lenses improved over the years, microscopes were made which could be used to see smaller and smaller objects more clearly. One of the fields in which these microscopes enabled great advances to be made was microbiology.

Above: In 1628, William Harvey discovered the vital role of the heart as a pump that circulates blood in the body.

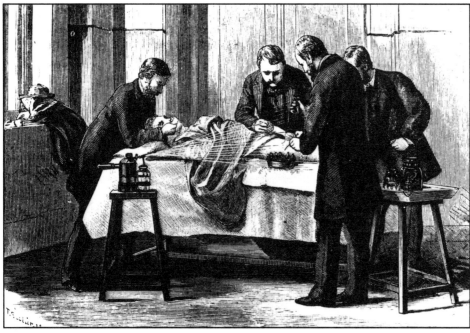

Left: A surgical operation in the 1860s. The patient has been anaesthetized with chloroform, which was first used in 1847.

FIRST MICROSCOPE MADE c.1600 • HOOKE AND LEEUWENHOEK DISCOVER CELLS 1665

MICROBIOLOGY

Below: In 1857 Louis Pasteur discovered that the air contains tiny living organisms, or microbes.

Microbiology is the study of tiny organisms such as bacteria and microbes. These organisms are too small to be seen with the naked eye, and microbiology only began after the invention of the microscope.

Louis Pasteur

The first person to discover micro-organisms was an Austrian doctor called Plenciz in 1762, but the real founder of microbiology was a French chemist, Louis Pasteur. In 1857 he was asked to find out why wine and other substances went bad when left exposed to the air. He discovered that the air contains tiny living things, which he called microbes. One of these, yeast, causes sugar to ferment into alcohol and makes bread rise. Others, germs or bacteria, make food go bad.

Pasteur also found that the microbes could be killed by heat, and much of the milk we drink today is heat-treated in this way, using a process called pasteurization.

Pasteur's discovery led on to the work of Joseph Lister, an English surgeon. He was appalled by the number of patients whose wounds became infected when the skin was broken, either in an accident or during surgery. Realizing that Pasteur's microbes might be responsible, from 1867 he devised methods of killing the germs responsible for infection and keeping them out of wounds. Without Lister's so-called anti-septic techniques, many of the surgical operations that we now take for granted would be impossible.

A German scientist, Robert Koch, made another important breakthrough in 1883, when he discovered the bacteria which cause two dangerous diseases in humans-tuberculosis and cholera. Further progress in the fight against disease came in 1898 when Martinus Beijerinck found micro-organisms that are even smaller than bacteria and can attack living cells from the inside. They are called viruses. Many viruses are too small to be seen even with an ordinary microscope, and could not be identified until the invention of the electron microscope in 1933.

The Battle Against Disease

As well as identifying the causes of serious diseases, scientists are also concerned about finding out how to

Right: Edward Jenner's use in 1786 of cowpox vaccine to prevent smallpox caused much hilarity. However, it was very successful, and smallpox has now been wiped out all over the world.

Below right: Joseph Lister, whose antiseptic techniques protected patients undergoing surgery against infections caused by germs.

cure or prevent them. The first important step in this direction came in 1786, even before the cause of the disease smallpox was known. An English doctor, Edward Jenner, noticed that people who had suffered from a mild form of smallpox, known as cowpox, never caught smallpox itself. He smeared a boy's arm with the liquid from cowpox blisters and then scratched the skin. Several months later he injected the boy with smallpox. The cowpox "vaccine" had made the boy immune to both cowpox and smallpox. Thanks to Jenner's discovery, smallpox has now been completely wiped out all over the world.

In 1885 Louis Pasteur vaccinated a man who had been bitten by a dog that had rabies. His experiment was a success and the man survived. Pasteur's contribution to the study of diseases did not end there. He suggested that humans and other living things had inside them cells that can fight diseases by attacking the microbes which cause them. Over the years he has been proved correct, and scientists are continually finding out more about the body's immune system.

JENNER VACCINATES AGAINST SMALLPOX 1786 • BEIJERINCK DISCOVERS VIRUSES 1898

GENETICS AND DNA

Have you ever noticed that children look like one or other of their parents in some ways? Perhaps you have some of the same characteristics as your own mother or father, the same colour eyes, similar facial features, or long or short fingers, for example. The passing-on of characteristics like these from parents to offspring is called heredity, and it is studied in the science of genetics.

Gregor Mendel

In 1866 Gregor Mendel, a monk in part of what is now Czechoslovakia, published the results of experiments he had carried out on garden pea plants. He had identified seven different characteristics, including shape of seed, colour of seed and length of stem, and had crossed plants with the same characteristics to see what sort of plants they produced.

At that time, it was believed that the offspring of animals or plants had characteristics halfway between those of their parents. Mendel proved otherwise. He found that when plants with tall stems were crossed

Below: Through his experiments with pea plants, Gregor Mendel discovered how physical characteristics are passed from parents to their offspring. The same principle can be seen in the diagram, which shows how eye colour is inherited.

with others having the same characteristic, most of the new plants would also have tall stems, but a quarter of them would have short stems.

His theory was that each characteristic is decided by two particles which are present in each plant. In tall plants, for example, there is one particle producing tallness and another producing shortness, but the tallness particle is "dominant", or more likely to be passed on. Therefore, a tallness particle from one plant crossed with a similar particle from another will give rise to another tall plant. Likewise, a tallness particle crossed with a shortness particle will also give a tall plant, because tallness is dominant. But when two shortness particles come together, as they do once in every four crossings, they produce a short plant.

Genes and DNA

We now call these particles genes. This was the name given to them in 1910 by Thomas Hunt Morgan, an American who experimented on heredity among fruit flies in much the same way as Mendel had with peas. Genes are contained in thread-like structures called chromosomes, found in the nucleus at the centre of each living cell.

The remaining mystery was how the information contained in genes of parents is passed on to their

MOTHER

● RECESSIVE GENE

● DOMINANT GENE

FATHER

CHILDREN

MENDEL'S EXPERIMENTS ON HEREDITY 1856-65 • MORGAN NAMES GENES 1910

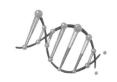

Below: When a cell divides, its DNA breaks down to form matched pairs of chromosomes.

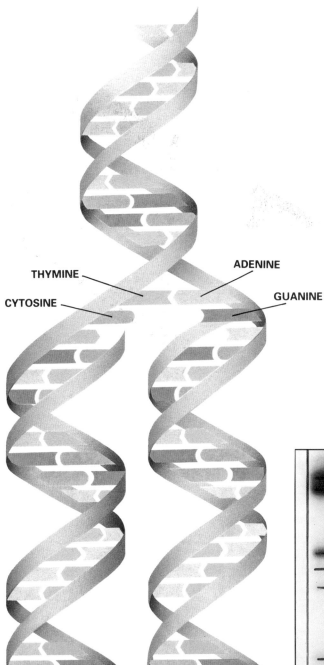

THYMINE

CYTOSINE

ADENINE

GUANINE

offspring. This question was solved in 1953 by Francis Crick and James Watson. They looked closely at a complicated molecule called deoxyribonucleic acid, or DNA, from which chromosomes are made. They found that it consists of long chains, each in the form of two interlocking spirals, made up of four different chemicals. Genes are made up of groups of these chemicals arranged in specific positions.

Living cells multiply by dividing in two. Each half becomes a new cell which grows and divides again. When a cell divides, the DNA in the nucleus breaks down and forms paired segments, chromosomes. All cells, except those responsible for reproduction, contain paired sets of chromosomes which carry all the information that is needed to make a particular organism. The reproduction cells contain only half of the information needed, and the complete "picture" can only be made by combining one cell from a male with one from a female.

The DNA of every individual animal and plant is different from all others. Because of this, scientists can now identify people by examining the DNA in, for example, their blood cells. This technique, called genetic fingerprinting, was developed in Britain in 1985 by Alec Jeffreys.

Below: Genetic fingerprinting; the pattern of bands is different for everyone, but people who are related have some similar bands.

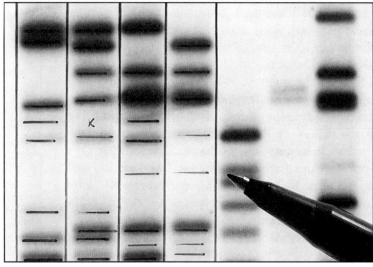

MODERN INNOVATIONS

During the last hundred years or so, medicine has advanced in leaps and bounds. Scientists and doctors have been able to find out exactly how diseases and other ailments affect the body, and have devised new methods of detecting, treating, and curing many of them.

One of the most well-known inventions is a drug called acetylsalicylic acid, or aspirin. It was first made in 1853, but was not recognized as a pain-killer until 40 years later. Furthermore, doctors have discovered recently that aspirin is also good for the heart if taken in moderate quantities.

Another invention benefiting the heart was made in 1958. The pacemaker, devised by Swedish doctor Ake Senning, can be implanted into a heart that is not beating correctly. The device supplies tiny electrical impulses to make the heart beat evenly and at the correct speed.

Sometimes the heart can become diseased. In exceptional cases, the disease may become so severe that the heart can no longer function, and doctors may carry out a heart transplant operation. This involves removing the diseased heart and replacing it with a healthy one from a suitable donor. The first heart transplant was carried out in 1967 by Dr Christiaan Barnard. It is also possible to transplant other organs, including the liver and kidneys.

Some of the most frequently used drugs are antibiotics. Made from micro-organisms, they work by attacking and destroying other micro-organisms, the bacteria and fungi that cause diseases. The first antibiotic, penicillin, was discovered by Alexander Fleming in 1928.

Medical Detectives

Röntgen's discovery of X-rays in 1895 immediately found a use in medicine. Because these rays pass through body tissue more easily than bone, it is possible to see broken or damaged bones in X-ray "photographs". In recent years, machines called scanners have been developed which can be used to view internal organs. The X-ray scanner was perfected in 1972 by Godfrey Hounsfield. Other types of scanner use radio waves or ultrasound (high-frequency sound waves). Ultrasound scanners are often used to examine unborn babies in the mother's womb.

Below: An operation to insert a heart pacemaker.

Bottom: An electrocardiogram is a type of graph that shows the tiny electric currents which make our hearts beat.

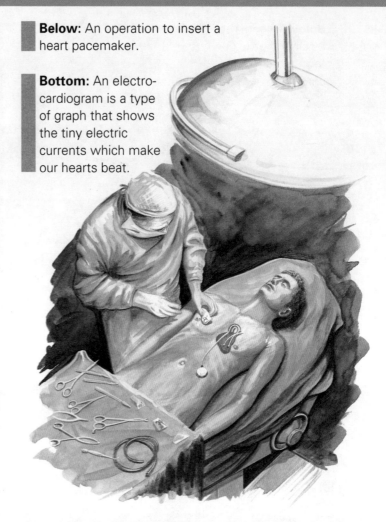

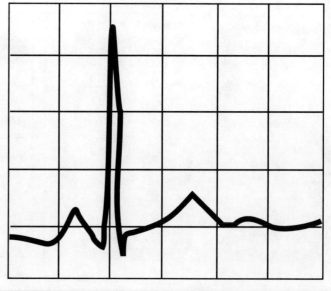

ASPIRIN FIRST USED 1893 • PENICILLIN 1928 • RADIOTHERAPY 1934 • PACEMAKER 1958

The Fight Against Cancer

There are a number of different types of cancer, affecting various parts of the body, but they all damage the body in much the same way. When an abnormal cell forms in the body, it sometimes multiplies quickly to form a tumour. If the tumour grows large enough, it can prevent an internal organ from working. Cancer cells can break free from a tumour and travel through the bloodstream to other parts of the body, where they start new tumours.

Until the discovery of X-rays, and of artificial radioactivity in 1934, there was no method of treating cancer. Doctors can now kill cancer cells by bombarding them with X-rays and gamma rays, which are aimed very carefully so that few healthy cells are damaged at the same time. This technique, known as radiotherapy, was first used effectively in 1934.

Another means of killing tumours was developed in 1964. It is called chemotherapy, and involves using very strong drugs to attack the cancer cells. Thanks to these two treatments, most cancers can now be cured if they are detected early enough.

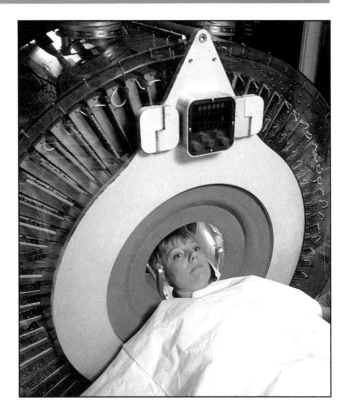

Above: A patient undergoing a brain scan. Scanners like this are often used to detect tumours in the brain.

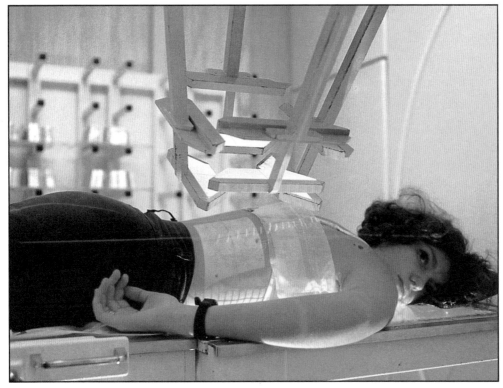

Left: Laser beams are used to ensure that a patient's body is positioned correctly prior to radiotherapy.

MATHEMATICS

NUMBERS

Mathematics is the name for a group of sciences which includes algebra, geometry and calculus. It is concerned with the study of the quantity and shape of things, how much space they occupy, and the links between these factors.

Mathematics is vital to all other sciences, because it gives scientists a way of expressing their theories, recording and analysing the results of experiments, and explaining their conclusions. Perhaps most important of all is the fact that the "language" of mathematics (the signs and symbols that are used and the way in which calculations are written down) is international: one scientist can read and understand the mathematical calculations of another, even though they may live on opposite sides of the world and be unable to speak each other's language.

The First Numbers

Numbers have a central part to play in the language of mathematics. The quantity of something is expressed as a number: mass, speed, height and many other ways of describing objects are written as a number and a unit of measurement, 25g, 200 km/h, 46 m, for example.

Numbers were first used in writing about 5,000 years ago. Clay tablets found in the ruins of ancient cities in Mesopotamia and Persia are inscribed with symbols representing both words and numbers. From around 500 BC, the Mayan civilization in Central America developed a number system based on counting in twenties, the combined number of fingers and toes. At about the same time, the ancient Greeks began using the letters of the alphabet to represent numbers. Their system was used for a thousand years, and was adapted by both the Hebrews and the Arabs.

In Babylonia during the fourth century BC, a new symbol began to appear, the symbol for zero. Until then, the idea of there being none of something was represented by a space in a row or column of figures.

In the third century BC, certain special numbers were discovered by the Greeks. The mathematician Euclid realized that there were some numbers, called prime numbers, which can only be divided by 1 and themselves. For example, the only whole numbers (not

MODERN ARABIC	1	2	3	4	5	6	7	8	9	10	100
EGYPTIAN	I	II	III	IIII	II/II	III/III	IIII/III	IIII/IIII	III/III/III	∩	℮
HINDU	?	૨	३	४	५	૬	૭	૮	૯	?°	?°°
BABYLONIAN	▼	▼▼	▼▼▼	▼▼▼▼	▼▼▼/▼▼	▼▼▼/▼▼▼	▼▼▼▼/▼▼▼	▼▼▼▼/▼▼▼▼	▼▼▼▼▼/▼▼▼▼	►	▼◄=
ROMAN	I	II	III	IIII	V	VI	VII	VIII	IX	X	C
MAYAN	•	••	•••	••••	—	•/—	••/—	•••/—	••••/—	—/—	⬭

FIRST WRITTEN NUMBERS 5,000 YEARS AGO • ZERO FIRST USED FOURTH CENTURY BC

74

fractions) by which 11 can be divided are 1 and 11 itself. Therefore 11 is a prime number whereas 12, which can be divided by 1, 2, 3, 4, 6 and 12, is not. The largest prime number so far discovered was found by accident in 1985, with the aid of a supercomputer. It is a staggering 65,050 digits long.

The Modern System

The development of our modern system of numbers began in India around 1,500 years ago. For the first time, numbers were represented by just ten figures, from 0 to 9, as used today. Numbers greater than 9 were shown by combining figures and placing them in what are called decimal positions. For example, in the number 2,365, the right-hand position shows single units (ones), the next position is for tens, the next for hundreds, and so on.

In 829 the Arab scientist Mohammad Ibn Musa al-Khwarizmi adopted this system, and its use was later spread to Europe. However, the ten figures were not always written in the same way. When the printing press was invented around 1440, it was possible to fix the exact shapes of the figures so that everyone used the same ones.

Below: Roman numerals are very popular. Here we see them used on a clock face.

Left: Some examples of ancient number systems, together with the equivalent arabic numerals we use today.

GEOMETRY

We saw in the previous chapter how numbers were first used and how our modern number system was developed. The area of mathematics which deals with numbers and numerical calculations (addition, subtraction, multiplication and division) is called arithmetic. If you look around, you will see that the world consists not of numbers but of shapes, which are made up of straight lines, curves and surfaces. The study of these shapes is called geometry.

Early Geometry

The earliest practical uses of geometry were in building. When a temple, for example, was being constructed, its builders needed to know whether or not the ground was level and the walls vertical. From the time of the world's first cities, which grew up around 5,500 years ago, builders have used devices such as set squares (triangles in which one angle is a right angle) to help them build walls at 90° to the ground. The ancient Egyptians knew how to make a number of these right-angled triangles, with sides of various lengths. (The simplest has sides of 3, 4 and 5 units.) The Babylonians probably knew many more.

In the seventh century BC, the Greek mathematician Thales devised a clever way of measuring the height of buildings and other objects. He measured the shadow cast by the object when the sun was at an angle of 45°(half of a right angle) in the sky, because he had calculated that the length of the shadow would then be the same as the height of the object.

Pythagoras and Euclid

The person who did most to advance the science of geometry was Pythagoras, a Greek mathematician of the sixth century BC. He looked at right-angled triangles and asked himself what makes them special. What is the relationship between the lengths of the three sides? The answer he arrived at is known as Pythagoras' Theorem. It states that "the square of the hypotenuse is equal to the sum of the squares on the other two sides". Or, to put it more simply, if the length of the hypotenuse (the longest side of the triangle which faces the right angle) is squared (multiplied by itself), the number this makes will equal the square of one of the remaining sides added to the square of the other. In a simple 3,4,5 right-angled triangle, for example, the hypotenuse is 5 units long. When it is squared (5 x 5)

it makes 25. The squares of the other two sides are 9 (3 x 3) and 16 (4 x 4), which add up to 25. Pythagoras' Theorem is true for every triangle that contains a right angle, and it has been called the most important single theorem in the whole of mathematics.

One of the most famous names in geometry is that of Euclid, a Greek who lived in Alexandria from about 300 BC. He gathered together the work of earlier mathematicians, including Pythagoras, and organized it into an orderly system. His book, *Elements of Geometry*, has been translated and copied more times than any other book apart from the Bible. It was still being used to teach geometry at the beginning of this century.

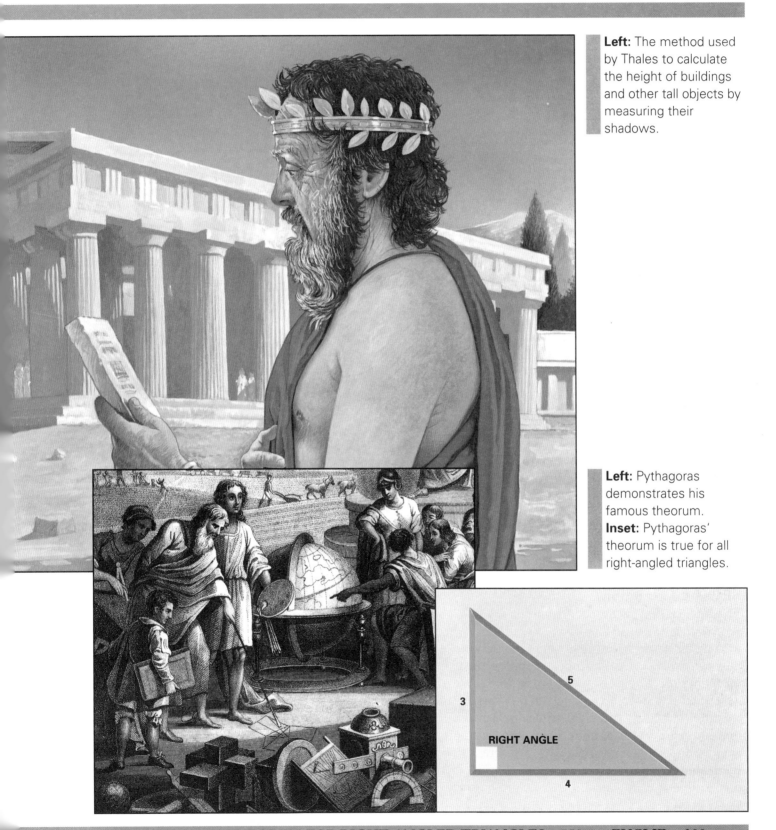

Left: The method used
by Thales to calculate
the height of buildings
and other tall objects by
measuring their
shadows.

Left: Pythagoras
demonstrates his
famous theorum.
Inset: Pythagoras'
theorum is true for all
right-angled triangles.

3

5

RIGHT ANGLE

4

PYTHAGORAS' THEOREM FOR RIGHT-ANGLED TRIANGLES c.550 BC • EUCLID c.300 BC

ALGEBRA

Algebra is a branch of mathematics. It is rather like a special language in which symbols are used to represent numbers and quantities. Many of these symbols are letters of the alphabet. These letters are often used to represent unknown quantities. Arithmetical signs, such as + and - for addition and subtraction, are also used, and so are ordinary numbers.

Signs and Equations

The ancient Egyptians had signs for addition and subtraction: in their hieroglyphic writing, two legs walking in the same direction meant the same as our plus sign, while two legs walking in opposite directions meant minus. The signs we use today were originally developed in the fifteenth, sixteenth and seventeenth centuries. Although the origins of algebra date back to the third century in Alexandria, Egypt, the first important developments were made by two Frenchmen, Pierre de Fermat and François Viète. In 1591, in his book *Ars analytica*, Viète first devised the language of algebra that is still used today.

Algebra is used as a means of describing the relationships between things, and using these relationships to calculate unknown quantities from known ones. This is done using what are called equations. These are rather like mathematical versions of the sentences you use when speaking, except that they contain numbers and letters instead of words. You might have guessed from the spelling of the word equation that it has something to do with being equal. Equations are written in such a way that the quantities on both sides are equal, as in a simple equation such as $n + 8 = 20$. The unknown quantity, n, can be calculated by solving the equation. In solving equations, you can use addition, subtraction, multiplication and division, but you must always do the same thing to both sides of an equation to make sure that they stay equal. The aim is to get the unknown quantity, n, on its own on one side of the equation. For example, to solve $n + 8 = 20$, you can subtract 8 from each side, making $n = 20 - 8$. You can then see that n equals 12.

ALGEBRA ORIGINATES IN THIRD-CENTURY ALEXANDRIA • FRANÇOIS VIÈTE (1540-1603)

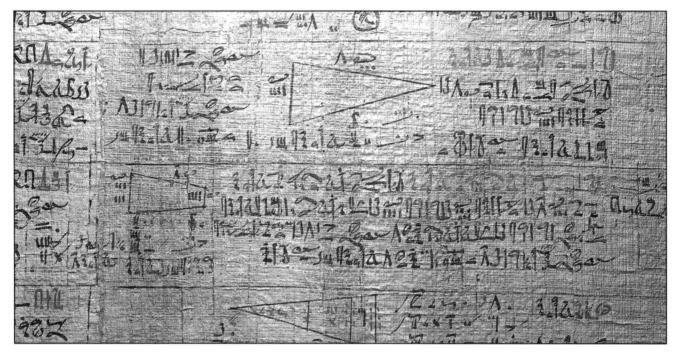

Above: Part of an Egyptian mathematical papyrus from about 1575 BC.

Below: François Viète (1540-1603) was the founder of modern algebra.

Solving Practical Problems

Equations can be used to solve problems in everyday life. Perhaps you are planning to go on a car journey with your parents. If the petrol tank holds x litres and the car can travel y kilometres for every litre, you will be able to go z kilometres before stopping for petrol. Each litre takes you y km and you have x litres, so you can go $x \times y$ km, which is written as xy. You know the distance is z, so you can write $xy = z$. So long as you know two of these three quantities, you can solve the equation. If x is 36 litres and y is 12 km per litre, $x \times y$, (which equals z) is 36 x 12, or 432 km. If your journey will be longer than 432 km, you will need more petrol.

You can also use equations to work out how much things cost. If a 5kg bag of potatoes costs a certain amount of money, you can calculate how much each kg costs, and compare it with the price of, say, a 3kg bag.

Many equations are much more complicated than the ones we have looked at, but they are just as useful when it comes to solving difficult problems in science.

LANGUAGE OF ALGEBRA DEVELOPED BY VIÈTE 1591 • PIERRE DE FERMAT (1601-1665)

THE
INDUSTRIAL
REVOLUTION

IRON AND STEEL

Nowadays, anyone looking down from a bridge at a crowded motorway with thousands of motor vehicles speeding by, will get some idea of mass production. In ancient and medieval times, a few things such as salt and glass bottles were mass-produced. More complicated mass production had to wait for the Industrial Revolution to provide the necessary power and quantities of metals and other materials.

Coke and Blast Furnaces

The Industrial Revolution began in the early eighteenth century when coke, a fuel made from coal, was first used to make iron metal from its ores. This new process was called smelting. Abraham Darby (1677-1717) of Shropshire first used coke fuel to smelt iron ores in a blast furnace. Coke burns more efficiently and at a higher temperature than coal. As a result, Darby's coke-fired blast furnaces were able to produce iron metal in much larger quantities than had

Below: An iron foundry at the beginning of the nineteenth century.

Right: A modern blast furnace like this makes hundreds of tonnes of pig iron each day.

COKE AND IRON ORE

HOT AIR BLAST

MOLTEN SLAG

MOLTEN IRON

DARBY SMELTS IRON ORE WITH COKE 1708 • DAVY INVENTS MINERS' LAMP 1815

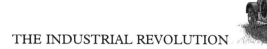

been possible in earlier, coal-fired blast furnaces.

With the greater amounts of iron available, much larger iron objects could be made. Abraham Darby's grandson, of the same name, built the world's first giant iron structure, a bridge, in 1779 (see page 87). Many complicated machines began to be made out of cast iron, including the steam engines we shall see on pages 84-85.

In England and other newly industrialized countries, coal mining increased greatly, providing more coke for the smoking blast furnaces. Coal mining was made safer in 1815 with the invention of the first miners' safety lamp by Sir Humphry Davy (1778-1829). The flame of this ingenious oil lamp burned inside a metal gauze shield, and would light a miner's way underground without causing explosions of mine gases.

The Age of Steel

Steel is an iron alloy containing a smaller and more precise quantity of carbon than cast iron. It is even tougher and stronger than cast iron, but was made in much smaller quantities until about 1870, when newly-invented types of blast furnace began to produce steel in batches of 25 tonnes or more.

One new steel furnace was the Bessemer Converter. It operated by blasting air not through the burning coke fuel as in Darby's blast furnace, but through the molten metal itself. This burned off most of the carbon in the metal, to make gases such as carbon monoxide. The gases bubbled up through the molten mass of metal and escaped from the furnace through a flue or chimney. By adjusting the air blast, a small but precise amount of carbon was left in the metal, just enough to make steel.

At the start of the twentieth century, everyone grew aware of the value of steel, as it became the new material for all sorts of machines, including motor cars. In 1908, Henry Ford in the USA invented mass production of motor cars with the manufacture of his Ford Model T family saloon.

Left: Stainless steel on a very large scale: the Thames Barrier in London, designed to prevent flooding.

MASS PRODUCTION OF STEEL FROM 1870 • MASS PRODUCTION OF CAR FROM 1908

STEAM POWER

Steam Pumps

In the Middle Ages, the power for turning a mill wheel was obtained from falling water, or from the wind, or from donkeys or other animals. Water-powered wheels were also used for pumping out flood water from coal and metal mine-workings. At the very end of the seventeenth century, many of these water-powered mine pumps were replaced by steam-powered pumps. Burning wood or coal to turn water into steam, these pumps were the earliest important industrial steam engines.

Thomas Savery (1650-1715) invented the first steam pump for mine drainage in 1698. A somewhat more efficient steam pump was invented by Thomas Newcomen (1663-1729) in 1705. These were both very large and clumsy machines. The pumping engine invented by a famous Scotsman, James Watt (1736-1819), in 1769, was much neater and more efficient. Another of Watt's important inventions was a governor, a device for controlling the speed of a steam engine. By 1782, Watt had designed further-improved steam engines of the sort to be used in only a few more years for the first steamboats and steam locomotives.

The Railway Age

Wagons running on rails, pulled by horses or pushed by men, had been employed since the 1500s for transporting coal and metal ores in mines. At first the rails were made of wood, then in the early 1700s, of iron. In 1804, the first steam locomotive to run on iron rails appeared. This was the invention of an Englishman, Richard Trevithick (1771-1833), who had previously built steam road carriages, which were less of a success.

Trevithick's steam locomotive of 1804 proved its worth by pulling five wagons filled with 10 tons of iron and 70 men a distance of five miles. It attained speeds of only a few km/h, but in 1829 the *Rocket* of George Stephenson (1781-1841) sped along on its rails at no less than 58 km/h. This famous little locomotive was of the type used on the first steam railway to carry both passengers and freight, the Liverpool and Manchester Railway of 1830.

Steamboats

In 1802, two years earlier even than Trevithick's first steam locomotive, the first successful steamboat came into operation. Named the *Charlotte Dundas*, she was powered by a new engine designed by James

NEWCOMEN'S STEAM PUMP

One of the earliest practical steam engines was the steam pump invented by Thomas Newcomen in 1705 to pump water out of flooded coal mines. It had a piston that was forced upwards by pressure of steam from a boiler. The steam was cooled and therefore condensed, creating a vacuum and allowing air pressure to force the piston down again. As the piston moved down, it dragged a pumping arm, which pulled water from the depths of the coal pit to the surface.

Right: From 1820 to 1870, the big Mississippi paddle steamboats dominated trade and social life in central USA.

FIRST STEAM PUMP 1698 • WATT'S STEAM ENGINE 1782 • STEPHENSON'S *ROCKET* 1829

Watt and constructed by William Symington of Glasgow, in Scotland.

The first steamboats, like many larger ones that later plied the waters of the Mississippi in the USA, were paddle steamers. The ship's screw propeller was invented in 1836 by an American, John Ericsson (1803-1889). From about 1850 onwards, most steam-powered boats and ships were propeller-driven. But often, they were built with masts and sails in case their steam engines broke down!

By the end of the nineteenth century, steamships included fighting ships and ocean liners built of steel. The fuel for their steam engines continued to be coal until the early 1900s, when oil fuel began to replace it. At the same time, a more efficient kind of steam engine, the steam turbine, began to be used in ships. Invented by an Ancient Greek more than 2,000 years before, it was only now proving really useful!

FIRST STEAMBOAT 1802 • SHIP'S PROPELLER 1836 • LARGE STEAM TURBINES BY 1900

ROADS AND BRIDGES

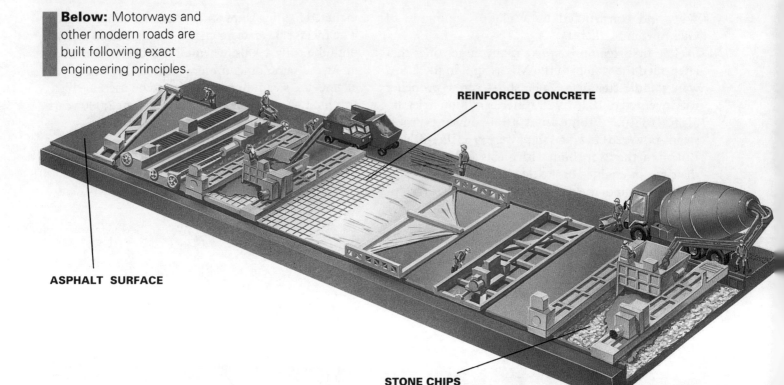

REINFORCED CONCRETE

ASPHALT SURFACE

STONE CHIPS

Roads

Among ancient road-makers, the Romans are famous for their arrow-straight roads. Roman road-makers first levelled the ground. Next, they laid down foundations of sand mixed with gravel or lime. Finally, they wedged stone slabs into this mixture to make the road surface. Sometimes, they cambered the road, that is they sloped it downwards at the edges. This caused rainwater to drain away so that the road did not become waterlogged.

This method of road-making sounds sophisticated, but crudely-slabbed Roman roads would soon ruin your shoes or bicycle wheels! In fact, roads remained crude constructions for a very long time. Even main roads of the nineteenth century in the most advanced countries often remained unpaved, and were muddy mires in wet weather.

Late in the nineteenth century, roads began to be paved with tarmacadam, a mixture of small stones bound together with tar, or the tarry substances asphalt or bitumen. This tarry surface dries hard, wears well, and is waterproof. Modern motorways and other major roads are constructed of reinforced concrete, with waterproofing layers either on top or below. The road may be electrically heated to melt any ice on its surface.

Tunnels and Canals

The longest tunnel of ancient times was 5.6 km long, dug through Mount Salviano in Italy with iron picks by Roman slaves. Tunnels of the nineteenth century reached 13 km long and were dug for railways. In 1861 pneumatic drills, operated by compressed air, were first employed for tunnelling, after explosives had been used to remove larger amounts of rock.

Modern tunnels, such as the "Chunnel" linking England and France, are cut with huge tunnelling machines. The earliest of these, called a tunnelling shield, was invented in 1818 by the famous British engineer Isambard Kingdom Brunel (1806-1859). His railway tunnels were lined with brick, whereas modern tunnels use reinforced concrete.

The earliest canals, or man-made waterways, were dug out by the Ancient Mesopotamians 5,000 years ago. About AD 100, the Chinese invented the

---

FIRST ALL-METAL BRIDGE 1779 • PNEUMATIC DRILL 1861• ALPINE TUNNEL 1871

first locks to connect stretches of a canal at different levels. This allowed canals, and boats on them, to travel across sloping ground. Famous modern ship canals include the Suez Canal, opened in 1869, and the Panama Canal, opened in 1914.

Bridges

Wooden, stone, and rope bridges date from ancient times. The first all-metal bridge still spans the River Severn at Ironbridge, Shropshire. Erected in 1779, it is built entirely of iron made in the first blast furnaces of the Industrial Revolution.

Most metal bridges date from much later in the twentieth century. They are built from steel, together with reinforced concrete, which itself contains strengthening steel bars. The various types of large bridge include beam bridges, arch bridges, suspension bridges, and cantilever bridges. One of the longest bridges in the world is the Lake Ponchartrain Causeway in Louisiana, USA, which extends for more than 38 km.

Above: Abraham Darby's iron bridge over the River Severn, which was built in 1779.

Below: A giant tunnelling machine cutting the Channel Tunnel or "Chunnel".

TEXTILES

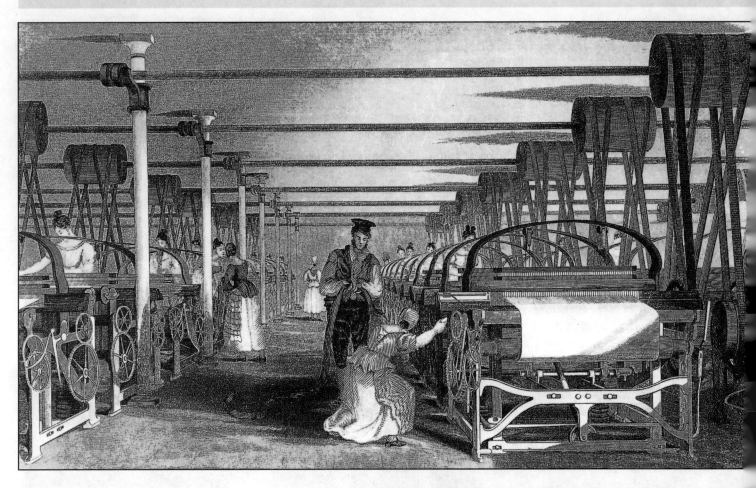

Above: A cotton-weaving factory in England, 1835.

Spinning, Weaving, and Knitting

Clothes-making is almost as old as humankind. In the traditional process, textiles for clothes, carpets, and hangings are woven from plant fibres such as cotton, or animal fibres such as wool. First, these fibres have to be drawn out and twisted to make yarn or thread. Then, cloth is woven using a loom, which interweaves the threads.

In very early times, threads were spun with a simple hand-held wooden instrument called a distaff and spindle. In the early 1300s the spinning wheel appeared, which speeded this process up. The spinning wheel was the ancestor of many later spinning machines. These included the spinning jenny, invented by James Hargreaves in 1764, the spinning

SPINNING WHEEL INVENTED c.1300 • SPINNING JENNY 1764 • SPINNING MULE 1779

frame, invented by Richard Arkwright in 1769, and the spinning mule, invented by Samuel Crompton in 1779. These machines spun several yarns at the same time.

The loom was improved by the invention, by John Kay in 1733, of the flying shuttle, which speeded up the interweaving process. Steam-powered looms date from 1787 when one was invented by Edmund Cartwright. All these British inventions had the effect of creating the first large cotton cloth industry, which was based in Lancashire. From the early nineteenth century, cloth-making from cotton took place in factory rooms containing rows of spinning machines and mechanized looms.

Knitting is another way of making cloth and garments. The first knitting machine, built around 1600, was called, for an obvious reason, the stocking frame. The first factory-operated knitting machines were used for lace-making in Nottingham in the early 1800s.

Dyes

Clothes and other textiles are nearly always dyed in suitable colours before being sold in the shops. Early cloth dyes were mostly coloured substances obtained from plants, such as indigo (blue), madder (red), and saffron (yellow).

Artificial or man-made dyes came into use much later. The first artificial dye was invented in the USA by William Perkin in 1856. Called mauvein, from its colour, it was made from aniline, a chemical product of the coal tar industry. This and the later petroleum industry have given us most of our modern dyes.

Synthetic Textiles

The label on an item of clothing often tells us that the garment is made fully, or partly, of a synthetic fibre such as nylon or terylene. These and other synthetic fibres are products of the plastics industry, which grew in size and production after World War II. Plastics are manufactured chemically by a process called polymerization, which combines small chemical molecules together to make giant molecules, or polymers. From the polymers, synthetic fibres are obtained by a spinning process rather like that used by a spider.

Synthetic fibres such as nylon are much stronger

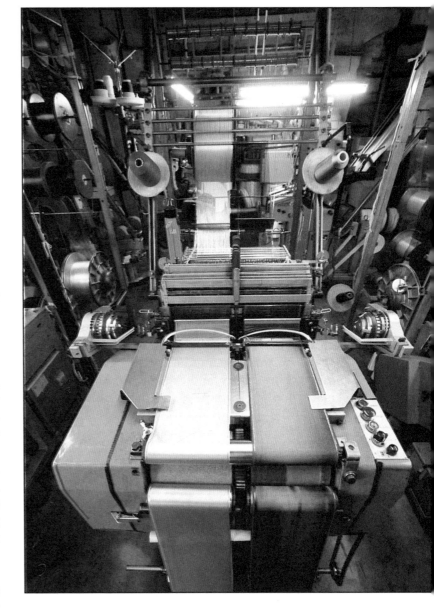

Above: Modern textile machines produce natural and synthetic fabrics at high speed.
Far left: Hand-dyeing cloth with indigo in Nigeria.

than natural plant fibres, and synthetic garments are harder-wearing - though many people still prefer cotton to nylon! Like natural fibres, synthetic fibres can be dyed a wide range of colours.

FLYING SHUTTLE INVENTED 1733 • SYNTHETIC DYE 1856 • NYLON 1930

THE NEW AGRICULTURE

Ploughing and Sowing

Medieval farming proceeded as it had for a thousand years past, with small farmers using primitive tools. One of the few great improvements was the use of a mould board on the plough. This turned over the ploughed soil more efficiently, so aerating the soil more and increasing its fertility. The mould board was invented by the Ancient Chinese but was not used by Western farmers before AD 1000.

Seed was scattered or sowed into ploughed furrows by hand. Early in the seventeenth century, seeding machines began to be used for planting seeds automatically. The best known of these is the seed drill invented in about 1701 by Jethro Tull (1674-1741) in Oxfordshire. This and later seeding machines planted a quantity of manure or other fertilizer at the same time as the seed, in order to help plants grow.

Jethro Tull is also credited with the invention of an early harrow for rooting up weeds and loosening soil. Harrows began to be used widely in the early nineteenth century, and can still be seen in country places today. Typically, they have a heavy metal frame with spikes or sharp-edged discs for disturb-ing the soil, and are dragged along either by a horse or a tractor.

Harvesting and Threshing

Farmers went on reaping their wheat or barley with sickles and scythes up until the late eighteenth century, when the first reaping machines were invented. In England, Henry Ogle's reaping machine of 1822

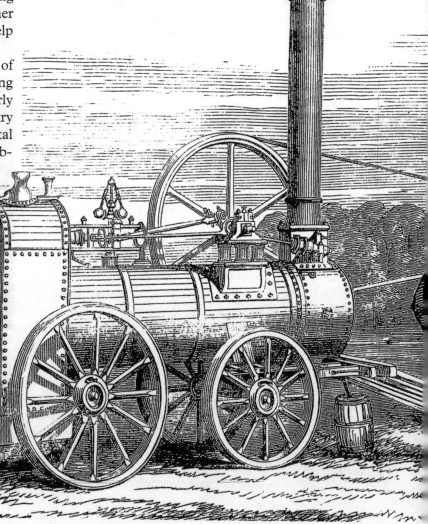

Right: A threshing machine of the 1850s. It is driven by a steam engine.

had a knife-blade to cut the crop and a reel of revolving bars to push the cut crop on to a platform.

To thresh grain, or beat it out from its husk, farmers had for countless centuries used a hand-held flail. The first threshing machine, which also featured a sort of flail, was invented by a Scotsman, Andrew Meikle, in 1786.

Combine harvesters, or combines, are so called because they combine both reaping and threshing. In addition, they automatically bind up stalks into bundles for haystacks or other forms of storage. The first combine harvester was invented by an American, Samuel Lane, in 1828.

These first combines were drawn behind horses. Later, larger, combines were steam-powered. Modern combines include giant diesel- or petrol-engined machines such as those that harvest the wheatlands of the USA. Special machines have also been invented for harvesting other crops, including cotton, potatoes, sugar cane, sugar beet, peanuts, and various fruits.

Intensive Farming

Since World War II, advanced methods of farming have led to intensive culture of plants and animals. Single crops of wheat are grown on a huge scale, with much use of artificial fertilizers and pesticides. In battery farming, tens of thousands of chickens may be kept in a single shed and fed automatically. Cows may never leave their indoor stalls, where they are fed and milked by automatic machinery.

THRESHING MACHINE INVENTED 1786 • COMBINE HARVESTER 1828

THE
ELECTRIC
AGE

ELECTRICITY

We owe our modern world of technology and industry mainly to steel and electricity. Both of these began to be made in large quantities in the late nineteenth century. The development of electric power came about after vital discoveries earlier in the century. The most important of these occurred when, in 1831, the great British scientist Michael

Faraday (1791-1867) invented a machine for making electric current - the first electric generator.

Electric Power Stations

From Faraday's small laboratory invention arose the giant electric generators of today's power stations. The first power station to provide electricity to houses and street lamps was the work of Thomas

Below: Thomas Edison in his laboratory. In front of him is one of his many inventions, an electric pen.

Edison (1847-1931), the great American inventor. In 1882 his electric power station started operation in the Pearl Street District of New York, USA.

Power stations feature another invention of Michael Faraday's, the electric transformer. This is a device for altering electric voltage and current from one level to another. In power stations, transformers raise the voltage of electricity supplied by generators to the very high voltage needed for distributing the electricity over long distances on the pylons and cables of the electric grid.

Electric Motors and Lamps

Faraday also invented the electric motor, a sort of electric generator in reverse. Electric current is supplied to the motor, which then supplies mechanical power to wheels or other moving parts. Electric motors are used to power a host of machines, from electric shavers to railway locomotives.

Another revolutionary invention of Thomas Edison, in 1879, was the incandescent filament lamp, or light bulb, which brought electric light into homes all over the world.

Electric Cells

Electricity can also be created by chemical reactions. Any device which stores chemical energy and delivers electric current is called an electric cell or battery. An early electric battery was invented in 1792 by the Italian Alessandro Volta (1745-1827). Modern chemical batteries include the familiar car battery or accumulator, and smaller dry batteries for electric torches.

Fuel cells are a twentieth-century invention for providing electricity. They are devices that use a continuous supply of fuel gases, which react together chemically. The energy of these chemical reactions is then produced as electric current. The uses of fuel cells include power packs in spacecraft.

Electric solar cells are another modern invention. They obtain their power from the Sun and convert this light energy directly into electricity. These cells are used in space research, and even more recently, large batteries of solar cells are becoming important for heating and lighting houses and a great variety of other buildings.

NON-POLLUTING POWER

Most electric power stations are polluting, but non-polluting power can be obtained in many ways:
1 By damming a lake or river, then releasing water through turbines, which generate electricity. **2** By damming a river estuary, then allowing water from the tides to flow through turbines. **3** By putting many small water turbines in the sea, each of which makes electricity from the waves. **4** By causing the wind to turn giant windmills or electric generators. **5** By using the power of sunlight, for example by converting its heat and light into electricity with banks of silicon cells. **6** By using heat in the Earth's crust to boil water to make steam. This is then used to operate steam turbo-generators to make electricity.

1 HYDROELECTRIC POWER

DAM

2 TIDAL POWER

HIGH TIDE

LOW TIDE

TURBINE

3 WAVE POWER

WAVE

4 WIND POWER

5 SOLAR POWER

BANKS OF SOLAR CELLS

6 GEOTHERMAL POWER

TELECOMMUNICATIONS

Below: In the late nineteenth century, messages began to be sent all over the world by telegraph.

To communicate with one another at considerable distances, people once had to rely on letters carried by land and sea. With the tremendous increase in trade and travel during the Industrial Revolution, businessmen and others needed to know more quickly what was happening, both at home and abroad. By the mid-nineteenth century, new discoveries and inventions in electricity (see pages 94-95) made this faster communication possible.

Telegraph and Morse Code

In 1837 in the USA, Samuel Morse invented the first telegraph, an instrument for sending electrical messages from one place to another through a wire cable. He also invented a code of long and short pulses of electricity, or "dashes and dots", known as the Morse Code, which was used to send these messages. Alfred Vail, who worked with Morse, invented a hand-operated metal contact lever or key for sending Morse-coded messages along the telegraph cable. In the 1850s, Morse's first long-distance electric telegraph began to operate over the 65 km distance between Baltimore and Washington in the USA.

Later telegraph cables were much longer than this, some extending for thousands of kilometres under the Atlantic and Pacific Oceans. Eventually, electric telegraph messages could be sent right round the world. To send these messages more efficiently, special typewriters called teleprinters were invented in the 1930s. Messages typed out at one end were almost immediately printed out automatically at the other. By this time, long-distance messages could also be transmitted without the need for a cable, by radio telegraphy (see pages 110-111).

Telephone

A telegraph message along a cable needs to be in code, but a telephone allows people to talk to each other directly. The telephone was invented in the USA in 1876 by Alexander Graham Bell, a Scots-born American. A year later, his invention was

ELECTRIC TELEGRAPH AND MORSE CODE INVENTED 1837 • BELL'S TELEPHONE 1876

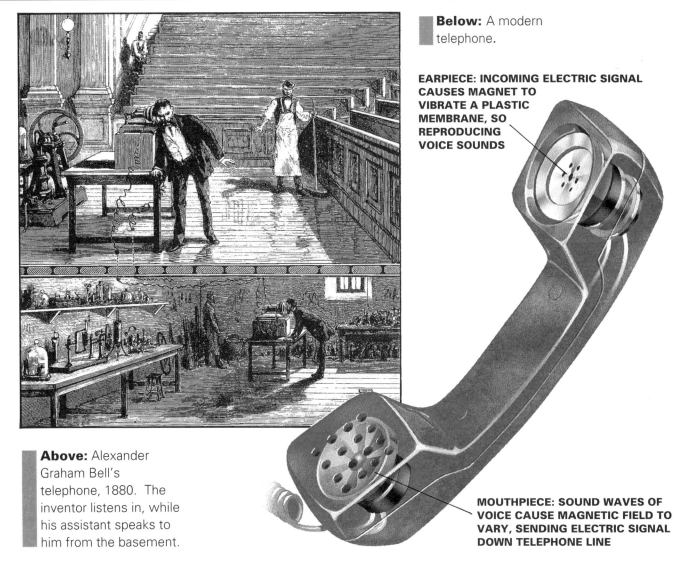

Below: A modern telephone.

EARPIECE: INCOMING ELECTRIC SIGNAL CAUSES MAGNET TO VIBRATE A PLASTIC MEMBRANE, SO REPRODUCING VOICE SOUNDS

Above: Alexander Graham Bell's telephone, 1880. The inventor listens in, while his assistant speaks to him from the basement.

MOUTHPIECE: SOUND WAVES OF VOICE CAUSE MAGNETIC FIELD TO VARY, SENDING ELECTRIC SIGNAL DOWN TELEPHONE LINE

improved by the American inventor, Thomas Edison.

Edison's improved telephone, like the telephones we use today, contained another new invention, the microphone. This has a diaphragm, rather like an eardrum, and an electromagnet connected to the telephone wire. Someone speaking into the microphone causes the diaphragm to vibrate, which in turn causes variations in an electric current flowing through the electromagnet. At the other end of the telephone wire, this varying electric current is turned back into sound, so reproducing the voice message.

The video telephone is a really new invention, using which people making and receiving a call can see, as well as hear, one another. The video telephone uses fibre optics (see pages 118-119) to carry the visual image.

Telemetry

By the 1930s, scientists were sending balloons high up into the Earth's atmosphere to record the weather. The weather balloons sent back their scientific data automatically, in the form of radio messages. Other man-made objects in the sky, such as aircraft, could be remote-controlled by radio signals. This is called telemetry. Examples of telemetry today include the control and relay of automatic messages from space satellites and probes.

TELEPRINTERS INVENTED 1930s • RADIO TELEMETRY FIRST USED 1930s

PHOTOGRAPHY

Before the nineteenth century, images of people and objects were mostly made by artists such as painters and sculptors. Another early means of creating an image, known since the time of the Ancient Greeks, was the camera obscura. This is basically a darkened room or box ("camera" means "room" in Latin) with a small hole in one wall to let in daylight. An image of the scene outside then appears on the opposite wall. Artists later made use of the camera obscura for such tasks as drawing outlines of objects and scenes in correct perspective.

Camera and Photograph

The camera obscura is the ancestor of the modern photographic camera, which is also basically a box with a hole in it. Fitted into the hole is a transparent lens to let in light. The light from an object falls on to a light-sensitive film, which then records the object's image, called a photograph.

Photography as a whole was not invented by any one person - many people made photographic discoveries and inventions. In 1725 a German chemist, Johann Schulze, showed that the chemical compound silver nitrate turned black when exposed to light. In 1816 a Frenchman, Nicéphore Niépce, obtained a blackish photographic image using paper immersed in a solution of silver chloride.

Niépce could not "fix" this image to make it stay on the paper. He achieved this later, in 1826, together with another Frenchman, Jacques Daguerre. The first satisfactory photographs, appearing in 1829, were called daguerreotypes after this last inventor. Daguerreotypes were positive photographic images, fixed directly on to a copper plate using sodium thiosulphate, a chemical compound still used in photographic fixers.

For most modern photographs, a negative image is first made, from which many positives can be reproduced. The inventor of the first type of negative-positive photography, in 1839, was an Englishman, William Fox Talbot. However, it took various experimenters another 50 years to produce the flexible rolls of photographic film we use today.

Black-and-White and Colour

In modern photography, a roll of photographic film, contained in a light-proof cassette, is first placed in

Below: In a modern reflex camera, light enters the lens and is reflected by a mirror and a prism into a viewfinder, showing the photographer the scene. A light-exposure meter tells the photographer what shutter speed and lens aperture (opening) he should use.

Below right: William Fox Talbot of England made this early box camera in the 1840s. He fitted it with a lens from his microscope and pinned light-sensitive paper onto the inside of the hinged back of the camera.

SHUTTER

EXPOSURE METER

MIRROR

FILM

NIEPCE'S FIRST PHOTOGRAPH 1816 • FIRST DAGUERREOTYPE 1829

a camera. For black-and-white photography, the film, made of a plastics material, is coated with a solution of silver bromide. When light is allowed into the camera by clicking the shutter, a negative or reversed black-and-white image is formed on the film. When the film is removed from the camera, a positive black-and-white image is produced on paper by developing and printing the film using various chemicals. This positive print is the photograph.

In colour photography, the photographic film contains chemical dyes sensitive to coloured light.

The first modern colour negative films were made in the 1930s. Like black-and-white negatives, these films need to be developed and printed to make the final photograph. Modern colour slides or transparencies were introduced later, in 1946. They only need to be developed to produce the final coloured photographic image.

The Polaroid camera has a special colour film that contains both dyes and developer, which are released when the shot is taken, producing a colour photograph, which is then pulled from the camera.

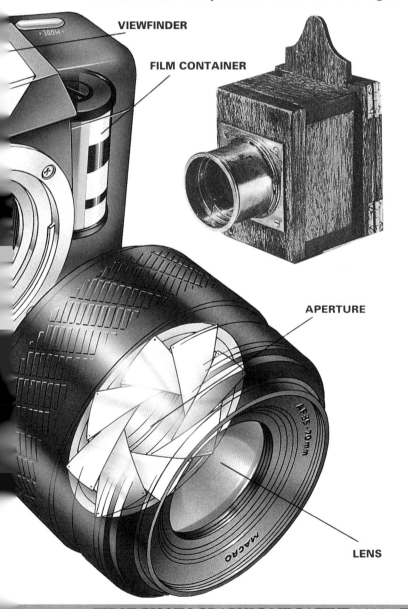

VIEWFINDER

FILM CONTAINER

APERTURE

LENS

MOVING PICTURES

The cinema shows us many photographs that follow one another so quickly that we see them not as separate pictures but as a continuous scene or action. The first cine-camera was invented by Etienne-Jules Marey in 1882. It was a gun camera that was first sighted on the object to be photographed, then took 12 photographs each second when the trigger was pulled. In more modern types of cine-camera, photographic film from a reel is fed through the camera while a shutter lets in and cuts off light at short intervals. The series of photographic negatives taken in this way is "played back" with a cinema projector, as the motion picture or film that we watch.

FIRST PHOTOGRAPHIC NEGATIVE 1839 • FIRST ROLL FILM 1885 • COLOUR FILM 1930s

HOUSEHOLD INVENTIONS

Electricity was first supplied to light people's homes in the early 1900s. It brought with it the possibility of many other domestic inventions. Most of these were labour saving devices. Others, such as radios and television sets (see pages 110-111) were more like luxuries. Labour-saving inventions gave people more time for listening and looking.

Cleaning

To remove dust from our homes we use a vacuum cleaner. A typical vacuum cleaner first brushes dust out of a carpet, then sucks it up with a suction fan rotated by an electric motor. Other fittings allow the vacuum cleaner to be used for cleaning curtains, cushions, and walls. The first vacuum cleaner was invented in 1901 by an American, Hubert Booth.

To clean our clothes we use a washing machine, also operated by an electric motor. Items to be washed go into a tub, together with a cupful of detergent or washing powder for loosening the dirt. In older-type machines, the motor turns or vibrates an agitator inside the tub to move the items around and wash the dirt out of them. In more recent washing machines, the motor spins the tub containing the washing. Washed clothes are dried either in a separate, electrically-heated drier, or automatically in the washing tub itself. The first electrically-powered washing machines date from just after World War I, but fully automatic machines were not manufactured and sold before 1937.

Sewing Machine and Safety Pin

Many families own a sewing machine for mending and making clothes. The first successful domestic sewing machine was invented in 1844 by Elias Howe in the USA. It was an improvement on an earlier machine of Walter Hunt, who, in 1849, also invented the safety pin.

Cooking and Storing Food

For cooking food we mainly use cookers heated by electricity or gas. Since the 1970s, microwave ovens have become popular. These cook food much more quickly because they heat up not the metal of the stove or pot but water in the food itself. The microwave was invented in the USA in 1945 by Percy Spenser for cooking popcorn.

For keeping food cool and fresh we use refrigera-tors and freezers. Nineteenth-century freezers were merely ice-boxes, but from the mid-twentieth century onwards, most household refrigerators had an electric motor. This pumps a cooling gas or liquid through pipes around the food.

Air Conditioning Homes

In countries that are cold some or all of the time, a modern house will be heated throughout by central heating. This can take the form of underfloor electric heaters, or heated air or water can be circulated through pipes and radiators. Heat for the air or water is provided by burning coal, oil, or gas in an electrically-controlled burner.

In hot countries a house may need to be cooled, and this is achieved with an air cooler, which refrigerates the air passing through it. Houses in countries with both hot and cold seasons may have a combined air-conditioning system.

Right: A modern house contains many gadgets for saving energy and making housework easier.

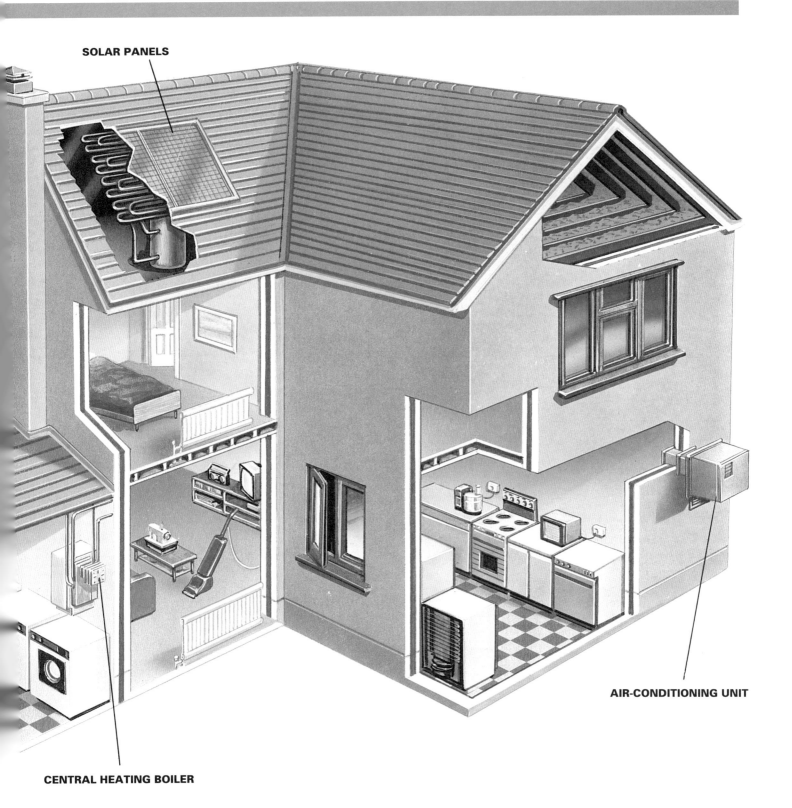

SOLAR PANELS

CENTRAL HEATING BOILER

AIR-CONDITIONING UNIT

CENTRAL HEATING INVENTED 1930s • MICROWAVE OVEN 1945

MODERN MEDICINE

Immunization

Perhaps the earliest invention of modern medicine was vaccination against the disease smallpox. This was first done as long ago as 1796, by an Englishman, Edward Jenner (1749-1823). The next form of vaccination came nearly 90 years later, when the great French scientist Louis Pasteur (1822-1895) vaccinated a boy against the terrible virus disease rabies in 1885. Thanks to these pioneers, we have vaccines today to protect or immunize us against many infectious diseases.

Surgical Operations

Operations were made far less painful by the invention of anaesthetics. In 1844 an American dentist, Horace Wells, first used nitrous oxide, or "laughing gas" as it was called, to make a patient less conscious of pain. At about the same time, the gas ether was used as a general anaesthetic to "put patients out" by two American doctors, Crawford W. Long and W.T.G. Morton.

In 1847 another famous early anaesthetic, chloroform, was first employed by a Scottish surgeon, James Simpson. In today's operations, these early general anaesthetics have been replaced by others which are less poisonous. Another safety invention for operations was the use of an antiseptic by an English surgeon, Joseph Lister (1827-1912). In the 1870s he used a spray of the antiseptic substance phenol, to kill any microbes that might infect surgical wounds. Lister's invention was the start of modern asepsis or microbe-free operating rooms.

Drugs against Disease

The earliest modern man-made drug was aspirin, which was first used in 1893 to relieve headaches and rheumatic pains. In 1910 the drug Salvarsan was invented by a German scientist, Paul Ehrlich (1854-1915). This was also known as "the magic bullet" because it was the first drug specially designed to cure a particular disease, syphilis.

In 1932, the first of a whole range of powerful

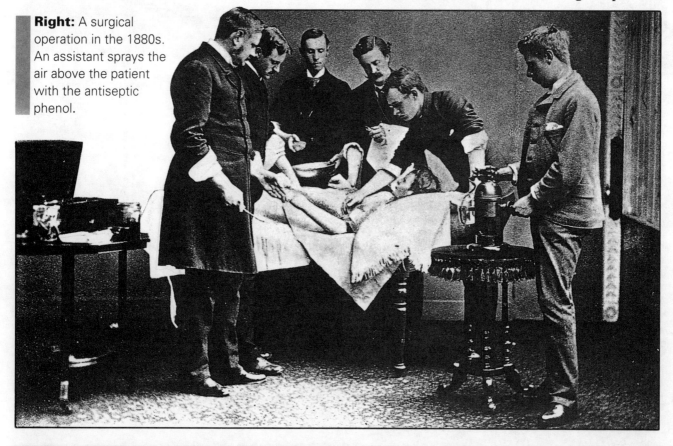

Right: A surgical operation in the 1880s. An assistant sprays the air above the patient with the antiseptic phenol.

microbe-killing drugs, the sulfa drugs, was invented by a German scientist, Gerhard Domagk. Sulfa drugs revolutionized the treatment of infectious disease, but were succeeded after World War II by the much less poisonous drugs called antibiotics.

Most famous of antibiotics is penicillin. This was discovered in 1928 by a Scotsman, Alexander Fleming (1881-1955), but was first manufactured and used to treat sufferers in 1941 by two other scientists working in Britain, Howard Florey and Ernst Chain.

Recent medical drugs include those designed to prevent a patient rejecting a new heart or other transplanted organ. Yet more new drugs have been invented to control mental illness, allowing patients to live normal lives outside mental hospitals.

Scanning Machines

X-rays, which penetrate solids such as the human body, were discovered in 1895 by the Dutch scientist Wilhelm Röntgen (1845-1923). In the early years of the twentieth century, the first X-ray ma-

Right: This modern X-ray machine scans a patient's brain to detect disease and other abnormalities.
Inset: A picture of the patient's brain appears on the monitor screen.

chines were invented for the examination, or scanning, of bones and other internal parts of the body.

More recent body scanners include ultrasound machines, which send out high-frequency sound waves and are used to examine babies still inside their mothers' wombs. Still other scanners are the ECG machine, which records details of heartbeat, and the EEG machine, which records electrical waves given out by the brain.

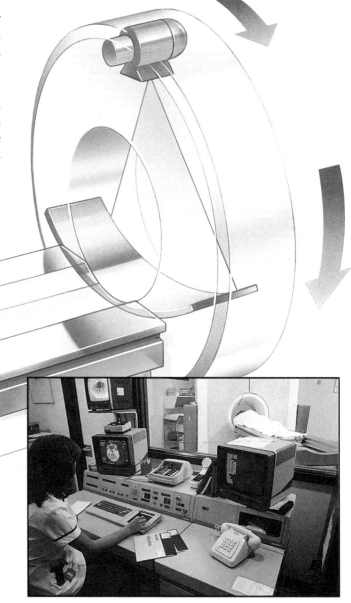

ROAD VEHICLES

The vast majority of cars, vans, and lorries we see on our crowded roads are powered by petrol or diesel engines. These are internal combustion engines, which get their power from explosions of fuel vapour or gas inside closed metal cylinders. The power of the explosions forces pistons up and down in the cylinders. This motion is transmitted, first to turn a crankshaft, and eventually to turn the vehicle's wheels. The ancestor of most modern internal combustion engines was invented in 1876 by a German engineer, Nikolaus Otto.

Another type of internal combustion engine was invented in 1956 by the German engineer Karl Wankel. The Wankel engine has no pistons. Instead, fuel vapour explosions cause a rotor to move around inside the engine casing. As in the Otto engine, this movement is then transmitted to the vehicle's wheels.

Motor Cars
The very first motor cars were also German inventions. They had petrol engines and were designed and built by Karl Benz and Gottlieb Daimler in 1885. Daimler and Benz soon became famous names in the world of motor cars.

Not long afterwards, the first diesel-engined cars appeared on the roads. The diesel engine was invented by Rudolf Diesel in Germany in 1897. In petrol engines, a mixture of fuel gas and air is exploded inside each cylinder by sparks from a spark plug. In diesel engines the gas-air mixture is exploded by pressure alone.

The first motor cars were luxury vehicles, built by hand in small workshops. For ordinary people to be able to afford them, motor cars had to be built more cheaply and in larger numbers. This was first achieved by Henry Ford in the USA in 1908. He invented the process whereby motor cars are assembled by many workers on a mass-production line. The Model T Ford, most famous of family cars, was mass-produced for 19 years until 1927.

Bicycles and Motorcycles
First ancestor of the bicycle was the "hobby horse", a crude two-wheeled vehicle "walked along" by young men-about-town, about the year 1815. The first

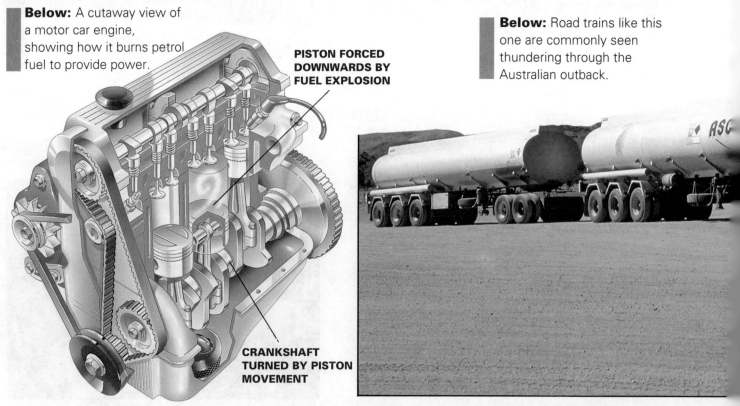

Below: A cutaway view of a motor car engine, showing how it burns petrol fuel to provide power.

PISTON FORCED DOWNWARDS BY FUEL EXPLOSION

CRANKSHAFT TURNED BY PISTON MOVEMENT

Below: Road trains like this one are commonly seen thundering through the Australian outback.

BICYCLE FROM 1815 • MOTORCYCLE FROM 1870 • ELECTRIC TRAM FROM c.1880

pedal-driven bicycle was invented in 1839 by a Scotsman, Kirkpatrick Macmillan. Inflatable rubber tyres were added later, having been invented in 1889 by a Northern Irishman, John Dunlop.

The first motorcycles, invented in France by Pierre and Ernest Michaux about 1870, were dangerously hot, steam-powered machines. Petrol-engined motorcycles were much safer. Earliest of these was a motor tricycle invented in 1884 by an Englishman, Edward Butler. A year later, a petrol-engined motor bicycle was built by the German inventor Gottlieb Daimler.

Electric Road Vehicles

Slow-moving milk floats are familiar electric vehicles on our roads, and small electric cars are becoming more popular as city runabouts. Such road vehicles are driven by an electric motor powered by a battery. Electric trams and buses are driven by engines powered from an overhead line. The electric road carriage was invented as long ago as 1837, by Robert Davidson, a Scottish engineer.

ELECTRIC CARS

Small electric cars like this French one are beginning to appear in our cities. They travel at reasonable speeds and, unlike most other road vehicles, do not pollute the atmosphere. Their power comes from an efficient electric battery, which at present can be used for a maximum of about 100 km, after which the owner must recharge the battery by plugging it into the electricity mains supply overnight.

PETROL-ENGINED MOTOR CAR 1885 • FORD MODEL T FAMILY SALOON CAR 1908

AIRCRAFT

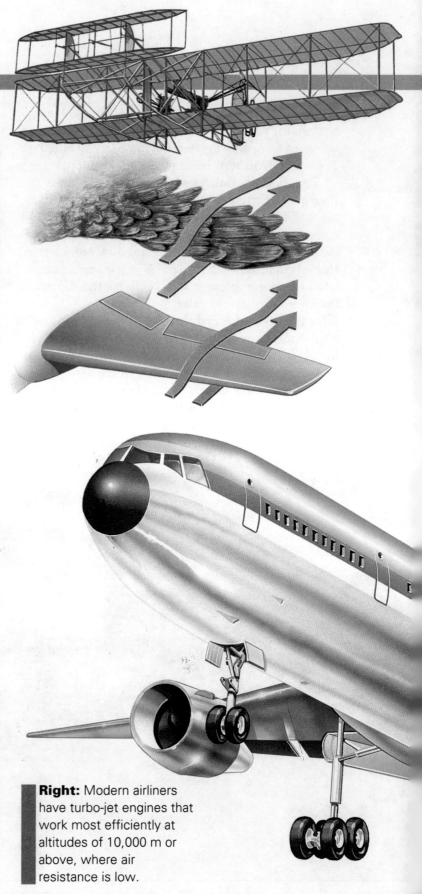

Balloons

Men first flew through the air when, in 1783, the Montgolfier brothers used a hot-air balloon to fly over Paris. Hot air weighs less than colder air, so that a balloon filled with hot air will rise up in the Earth's atmosphere. The balloon will then be driven along by the wind.

The Montgolfier brothers heated the air in their balloon with a fire in a bowl suspended beneath the open bottom end of the balloon. Hot-air ballooning is again popular today. Air in modern balloons is heated with a propane fuel gas burner supplied from a gas bottle.

In the early part of this century, balloons filled with hydrogen gas were more often seen. These included giant airships, called zeppelins, which bombed London in World War I. Hydrogen gas is much lighter than air, but it is also dangerously flammable. After a number of terrible disasters in which airships caught fire, a safer gas, helium, was used. Helium is the lightest gas after hydrogen, but it is very expensive. Because hydrogen was dangerous and helium expensive, giant airships soon became a thing of the past, though large gas-filled balloons are still used for such purposes as advertising.

Aeroplanes

An aeroplane is an aircraft that has wings or other structures that provide lift. When air passes across an aeroplane wing, the air pressure below the wing is higher than the pressure above the wing. This pressure difference increases as the aeroplane speeds up on the runway. When the pressure difference exceeds the weight of the aeroplane, the plane is lifted into the air, or takes off.

The earliest aeroplanes were model gliders. One built by Sir George Cayley (1773-1853) flew in England in 1804. In 1849 Cayley built a larger triplane, or three-winged glider, which carried a boy, the first person to fly in an aeroplane, a distance of a few metres.

The USA saw the real beginnings of modern aeroplane flight when in 1903, the brothers Orville and Wilbur Wright flew their petrol-engined biplane *Flyer 1* a distance of 260 m. Petrol-engined aeroplanes rapidly increased in size, speed, and safety.

Right: Modern airliners have turbo-jet engines that work most efficiently at altitudes of 10,000 m or above, where air resistance is low.

HOT-AIR BALLOON FLIGHT 1783 • WRIGHT BROTHERS' POWERED FLIGHT 1903

HOVERCRAFT

Hovercraft are really aircraft because they travel over water or land on a cushion of air. The air cushion is provided by turbines, which also turn propellers to push the hovercraft along.

Left: Air passing over and under the wings of an aircraft and a bird. The moving air provides lift, which keeps both plane and bird aloft.

Top left: The Wright *Flyer*, the first successful powered aeroplane.

Above: Helicopter blades act like revolving wings to provide lift, as shown in this French-made *Ecureuil*.

In 1909 Louis Blériot flew his monoplane from France to England across the English Channel. From large bombers used in World War I were developed the first airliners to carry passengers from country to country. Biggest of all were passenger seaplanes that took off and landed on water. The German Dornier Do-X seaplane of 1930 had 12 engines and carried 150 passengers at 400 km/h.

Jet Aeroplanes

The fastest and biggest aeroplanes today are powered by jet engines. Air enters the front of the engine and is used to burn fuel injected into the engine. The hot gases produced by this burning expand and blast out from the back of the engine, so thrusting the plane forward. In the 1930s, Frank Whittle in England developed the gas turbine jet engine that powered warplanes as well as post-war jets, but the first jet aeroplane of all to fly, in 1939, was the German Heinkel He 178.

BLERIOT FLIES ENGLISH CHANNEL 1909 • HEINKEL HE 178 JET PLANE FLIES 1939

SOUND RECORDING

Left: A piano recording being made in France in the 1880s. Thomas Edison's phonograph and some cumbersome "horns" are being used.

We hear sounds by means of air vibrations called sound waves which, in turn, cause our eardrums to vibrate. This is also the principle used to make gramophone records. An eardrum-like diaphragm is made to vibrate by sound waves. These vibrations cause a sharp stylus to cut grooves into a disc of plastics material. Sound can then be played back from the grooves, using another hard stylus, or needle. To be audible, the recorded sounds must be made louder, or amplified.

The inventor of sound recording, in 1877, was Thomas Edison (see also pages 94-97). His phonograph recorded sound as a pattern of little dents on a sheet of tinfoil. Ten years later, also in the USA, Emile Berliner invented a method of recording sound on rotating, spirally-grooved discs - the first gramophone records. Early recordings were made loud enough for people to hear by means of a trumpet-shaped amplifier.

Tape Recording

In 1898 a Danish engineer, Valdemar Poulsen, invented a method of recording an electrical signal in the form of patterns of magnetism on a metal wire. This method became the basis for magnetic sound recording, familiar to us as tape recording.

AMPLIFIER

MICROPHONE

SOUND

SOUND

Right: Making and playing an audio recording. The violin's sounds are picked up by the microphone and recorded on a cassette, which is played back through a loudspeaker.

Recording tapes are the work of many inventors, including J.A. O'Neil in the USA, who in 1927 invented a paper tape coated with a magnetic material. Modern tapes are made of flexible plastics coated with a material containing magnetic substances such as oxides of iron and chromium.

Tape recordings are made using a microphone (also invented by Thomas Edison) which converts sound waves into electrical signals. These signals then cause magnetic patterns to form on a magnetic tape. When the tape is played back on a tape machine, pick-up heads convert the magnetic pattern back into an electrical signal. The signal is amplified, then converted into sound waves.

The first modern electrical amplifier was the vacuum tube, or radio valve, invented in 1907 by Lee de Forest in the USA. The amplified electrical signal is fed into a loudspeaker, which contains an electromagnet. The signal causes this to vibrate, so producing sound waves.

Compact Disc Recording

In the early 1980s a new type of sound record began to be sold. The compact disc or CD is made of a plastics material, inside which is a spiral of very small "pits", lying at different depths. These have been cut out with a laser beam (see pages 118-119) in a recording studio. In a CD player, the compact disc is scanned by another laser beam which reflects from the non-pitted parts of the disc. The laser reflections are "read" by a light sensor which turns them into electrical signals. These are turned back into sound as in other types of sound or audio equipment. The great advantage of the compact disc is that the laser beam which is used for scanning causes absolutely no wear and tear, unlike a record player needle, or even the playing head of a tape player.

CDs are now also available for video recording of television programmes (see pages 110-111). In this process, both vision and sound are recorded on a compact disc.

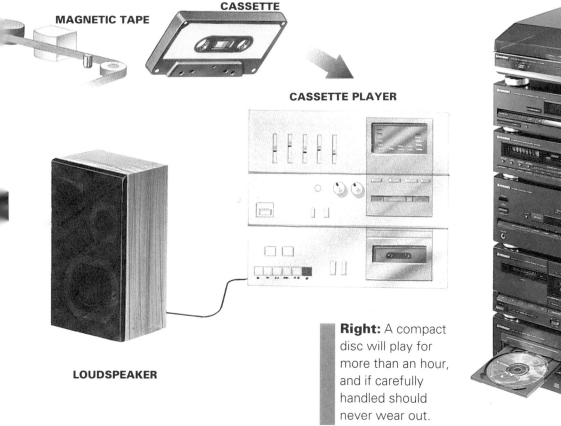

MAGNETIC TAPE

CASSETTE

CASSETTE PLAYER

LOUDSPEAKER

Right: A compact disc will play for more than an hour, and if carefully handled should never wear out.

RADIO AND TELEVISION

Radio

Radio waves were discovered in 1887 by Heinrich Hertz in Germany. He detected these waves with a metal wire loop in which the radio waves caused an electric current to flow. Hertz's wire loop was, in fact, the first radio receiving aerial or antenna.

The inventor of radio communication was an Italian, Guglielmo Marconi (1874-1937). In 1895, he used electric sparks to make radio waves travel outwards from an aerial. This was the first radio transmitter. Also, using a radio receiver like that discovered by Hertz, he detected his own radio wave signal at a distance of more than 1 km.

Marconi transmitted his radio messages in Morse Code (see pages 96-97). This was called wireless (radio) telegraphy - since, unlike earlier telegraphy, it needed no wire cable. By 1901 Marconi could transmit radio messages all the way across the Atlantic, and wireless telegraphy became important for passing code messages to and from ships at sea.

Even so, Marconi's early electric spark transmitter was a very inefficient way of making radio waves. The next leap ahead came with the invention in 1907 of the vacuum tube or radio valve (see pages 108-109). In an improved type of transmitter, radio valves

Above: Guglielmo Marconi, inventor of radio broadcasting.

amplified electrical signals to make more powerful radio waves.

Radio receivers were also greatly improved so that for the first time, human speech and musical sounds could be heard clearly. By the early 1920s, public radio broadcasting had begun, and people were beginning to listen in at home with their own "wireless sets".

Television

This form of public broadcasting transmits TV signals in the form of radio waves, which are received by the aerials of our TV sets, and turned into pictures on our screens. The first successful TV transmissions, in 1925, were those of a Scottish inventor, John Logie Baird. However, Baird's TV system was soon supplanted by another system based on a TV camera invented in the same year by Vladimir Zworykin in the USA.

In a TV studio, the scene to be broadcast is filmed with this special type of camera, which converts light signals into electrical signals. The signals are then

MARCONI INVENTS RADIO BROADCASTING 1895 • FIRST HOME RADIOS 1920s

amplified and transmitted as radio waves. At the same time, sound for the TV programme is recorded and also transmitted as radio waves. These waves are received by our TV aerials and turned back into sound and pictures in our TV sets.

A TV set contains a cathode ray tube, invented in 1897 by Karl Braun in Germany. The wider end of the cathode ray tube is the TV screen. Its narrower end, inside the TV set, contains a "gun" that fires a beam of electric particles, or electrons, at the screen. As they hit the screen, the electrons cause a special chemical coating, called a phosphor, to glow brightly.

The electron gun rapidly scans the TV screen from top to bottom. If there is no TV programme being received, an overall glow appears on the screen. An electrical TV signal modifies the intensity of the electron beam so that a picture appears on the screen.

Left: The inside of a colour TV set seen from the back. The red, blue, and green signals which combine to make the picture are directed onto the screen by three separate electron guns.

RADAR

The word RADAR stands for "RAdio Detection And Ranging". This means that radar can detect an object at a distance from us and also tell us how far away the object is. It does both these things by means of radio waves, which travel out from a radar aerial to hit the object and reflect back from it, to be detected by the aerial. The time taken by the waves to travel out and reflect back measures the distance of the object. An image of the object also appears on a radar screen, similar to a TV screen. Radar was invented in 1935 by Robert Watson-Watt, and used for defence against enemy aircraft in the Battle of Britain. Since that time, radar has also been used widely on ships and civilian aircraft.

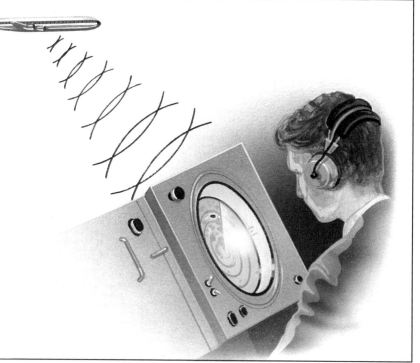

OIL AND GAS

Fossil Fuels

Like coal, petroleum oil and natural gas are fossil fuels. Coal was formed in the Earth's crust from trees and other plants that lived hundreds of millions of years ago. Similarly, oil and gas were formed in the Earth's crust from the decayed bodies of countless tiny creatures that once flourished near the surface of seas. All fossil fuels are known chemically as hydrocarbons because they consist largely of the chemical elements hydrogen and carbon. When they are burned in air, fossil fuels release both heat and the greenhouse gas, carbon dioxide.

Oil and Gas Prospecting

Petroleum oil is obtained mainly by drilling into the Earth's crust. The first oil well was drilled in Pennsylvania, USA, by Edwin Drake in 1859. To find out where oil lay, prospectors or explorers at first merely looked for where it seeped up to the Earth's surface.

At the beginning of the twentieth century, they began to look for much larger and deeper oil reserves by methods of geophysical prospecting. In one widely-used method, prospectors set off explosions on the surface, which send sound waves down into the Earth's crust. By examining the sound reflections from these explosions, geophysicists can tell where and at what depth oil lies.

By 1918, oil wells as deep as 6,000 m had been drilled. Modern drilling bits or cutters, at the end of the drilling stems or pipes, are tipped with extra-hard materials such as tungsten carbide or small diamonds, which cut through even the hardest rock. When oil is reached deep down, it is often under great pressure and pumps itself up to the surface.

Below: A dirty town gasworks in the mid-nineteenth century.

DRAKE'S FIRST OIL DRILLING RIG 1859 • OIL WELLS DRILLED 6,000 M DEEP BY 1918

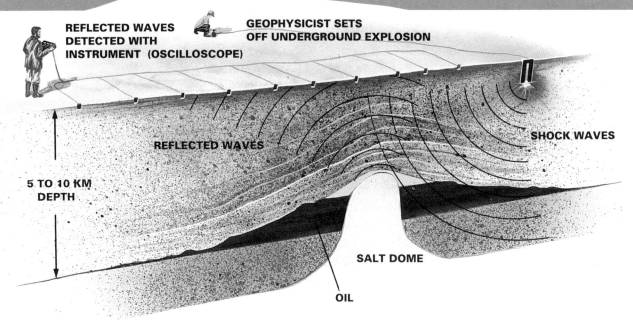

REFLECTED WAVES DETECTED WITH INSTRUMENT (OSCILLOSCOPE)

GEOPHYSICIST SETS OFF UNDERGROUND EXPLOSION

REFLECTED WAVES

SHOCK WAVES

5 TO 10 KM DEPTH

SALT DOME

OIL

Natural gas has been formed by similar processes to petroleum oil, and so is often found in the same places, under land or sea. For undersea oil or gas, huge drilling platforms are floated out to sea and anchored on the sea bed. Drilling then takes place in a similar way to land drilling. Natural gas consists mostly of the gas methane. It is piped away in huge volumes from the gas wells, both to industry and for burning in the cookers and gas heaters of our homes.

Petroleum Refining

Oil is pumped away from drilling rigs to be transported and refined. After World War II, bigger and bigger ships were built for transporting crude oil. A supertanker of today carries up to half a million tonnes. Crude oil is transported and pumped to an oil refinery, where it is heated and distilled to make a range of useful petroleum products. These distillation products may then be used more or less directly, as fuel oils for vehicle engines, such as petrol and diesel oil for road and rail vehicles, and as aviation fuel for aircraft. Similar refinery products include lubricating oils for reducing wear by friction in engines and other machines.

Other products of petroleum distillation are supplied to the chemical industry as raw materials. These are used to make a tremendous range of plastics, explosives, medical drugs, pesticides, synthetic fabrics, and pharmaceuticals.

Above: A simplified diagram of one geophysical method of prospecting for underground oil.

Below: An oil drilling platform off the Australian coast.

NUCLEAR POWER

All solids, liquids, and gases are made up of one or more types of chemical element, and 92 different elements occur in nature. Atoms are the smallest parts into which any chemical element can be divided or split up. A simple example is the element neon, the gas used in luminous signs, which consists solely of a mass of whirling neon atoms.

Splitting the Atom

The central part of an atom is called the nucleus, and this, too, can be split. The first scientist to split an atomic nucleus, in 1919, was an Englishman, Ernest Rutherford (1871-1937). He bombarded the gas nitrogen with sub-atomic "bullets" called alpha particles. They split the nuclei of many nitrogen atoms, turning these into atoms of another gas, oxygen. This process of splitting atomic nuclei is called nuclear fission.

The nuclei that Rutherford split also released energy in the form of very fast-moving sub-atomic particles, called protons. This is one example of nuclear energy. Another example is the nuclear radiation given off by atomic nuclei which spontaneously split up. Chemical elements having this unstable type of atom are said to be radioactive. They have many uses in science and technology.

Nuclear Reactors

Rutherford's discovery showed that atomic nuclei could release large amounts of energy. Scientists

Below: A cutaway view of a nuclear reactor used in the electricity generating industry.

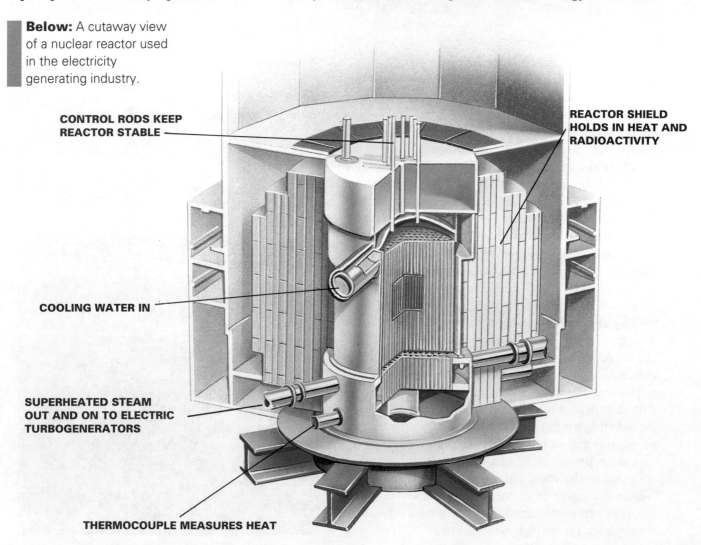

CONTROL RODS KEEP REACTOR STABLE

REACTOR SHIELD HOLDS IN HEAT AND RADIOACTIVITY

COOLING WATER IN

SUPERHEATED STEAM OUT AND ON TO ELECTRIC TURBOGENERATORS

THERMOCOUPLE MEASURES HEAT

RUTHERFORD SPLITS ATOM 1919 • FERMI BUILDS NUCLEAR REACTOR 1942

then began to ask how this energy could be produced and controlled on a large scale, to provide nuclear power. The answer came in 1942, when the Italian scientist Enrico Fermi (1901-1954) led a team in the building of the world's first nuclear reactor at the University of Chicago in the USA.

Nuclear reactors are the power units of nuclear power stations, which nowadays make a proportion of the world's electricity, and also provide nuclear explosives for weapons. In a nuclear reactor, energy is released from radioactive fuels in a controlled way. Heat made by the reactor is used to turn water into steam, which is then used to power steam turbogenerators that make electricity.

Below: Looking down into the cooling water of another type of nuclear reactor, the LIDO, at Harwell, England.

Thermonuclear Power

The Sun and other stars get their vast energy by another nuclear process, the combining together of atomic nuclei at temperatures of hundreds of millions of degrees. This thermal, or heated, combining of nuclei is called nuclear fusion, and the energy it produces, thermonuclear energy.

When nuclei of hydrogen atoms combine at these super-high temperatures, they form nuclei of atoms of the next heaviest gas, helium. However, some matter is left over, which turns into energy. As Albert Einstein (1879-1955) showed by his famous equation $e = mc^2$, even a tiny bit of matter turns into an enormous amount of energy.

Thermonuclear energy might provide all the power the world needs, if only it could be controlled. Inventions such as the *Tokamak* in the USSR, and *JET* in Europe are attempts to do this, but so far the only examples of man-made thermonuclear power are the devastating explosions of H-bombs.

Below: The *JET* experimental thermonuclear reactor.

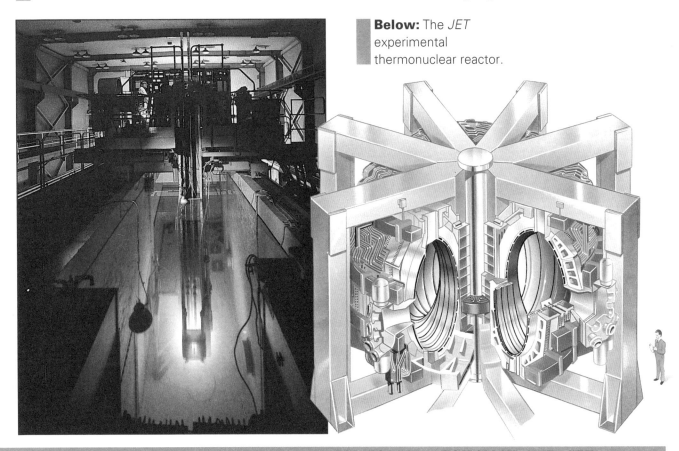

CHEMICAL INDUSTRY

Since the time of the Ancient Egyptians, people have made and used chemical substances. For thousands of years they have extracted salt from saltpans dried out in the sun, made glass from sand, and manufactured paints, pigments, and cosmetics - to give but a few examples of early chemical industry.

This chemistry, however, was always of a very practical kind. Useful substances were made without the scientific knowledge of just *how* they were made. The science of chemistry was often mixed up with the superstitions of alchemy. True chemical science had to wait until around 1766, when an Englishman, Henry Cavendish (1731-1810), made the first scientific description of the simplest of chemical substances, the gas hydrogen.

Large-Scale Chemistry

The earliest example of modern chemical industry was a large-scale process for making soda, or sodium carbonate, invented in 1787 by Nicolas Leblanc (1742-1806). The Leblanc process needed large volumes of another major chemical, sulphuric acid. This was quickly supplied by the lead chamber process, which was invented by a Scottish chemist, John Roebuck (1718-1794).

With the aid of these "bulk" chemicals, several more industrial chemicals were soon being made, including alkalis for large-scale soap manufacture, and hydrochloric acid, which was a by-product of this process. High explosives were another innovation of the mid-nineteenth century, with the discovery by A. Sobrero in 1846 of the violently explosive compound nitroglycerine, which was then used in 1866 by Alfred Nobel (1833-1896) to invent a much safer high explosive, dynamite.

Twentieth-Century Chemistry

A major chemical invention of the early twentieth century was the Haber process for making ammonia from hydrogen gas, together with nitrogen gas from the air. This process, invented in 1908 by a German, Fritz Haber (1868-1934), used an iron catalyst (a catalyst is a substance which speeds up chemical activity without itself changing) to make the gases combine. Both ammonia and metal catalysts became highly important for the next revolutionary chemical invention, plastics.

The first plastics material to be invented, in 1909, was bakelite, named after the Belgian chemist Leo Baekeland (1863-1944). Like other plastics, it is made by a polymerization process in which simple chemical substances, called monomers, are made to combine together to form very complex chemical substances called polymers or plastics.

Rubber is another important type of polymer. Since the early nineteenth century, natural rubber has been obtained from trees, but in 1910 a synthetic rubber was invented by the Russian, Sergei Lebedev (1874-1943). Both natural and synthetic rubber are used, for example, in motor car tyres.

Organic chemicals is the name given to an enormous number of chemical products, including dyes, inks, paints, solvents such as benzene, monomers for plastics, pesticides, perfumes, sweeteners such as saccharine, and medicines such as aspirin. These chemicals first began to be manufactured from coal tar in the mid-nineteenth century, and began to play a major part in industry in the twentieth century.

Below and right: This sulphuric acid plant burns the yellow sulphur in a furnace and converts the gases to acid with the aid of a metal catalyst.

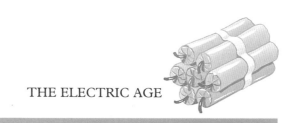

INDUSTRIAL CATALYSTS 1908 • FIRST PLASTICS 1909 • SYNTHETIC RUBBER 1910

SCIENTIFIC INSTRUMENTS

CHROMATOGRAPHY

Chromatography is a method used to discover what a chemical mixture is made of. In paper chromatography, the mixture is dissolved in a suitable liquid. Then a spot of this is placed near the lower edge of a strip of porous paper. The paper is hung so that this edge is immersed in a solvent liquid. The solvent rises up the paper, carrying the substances of the mixture with it, but the different substances rise at different rates, so that they separate out. Then, by various means, the identity and amount of each substance is calculated. Column chromatography works on the same principle, but instead of porous paper, uses a column of porous material in which the various substances in a mixture are made to separate out.

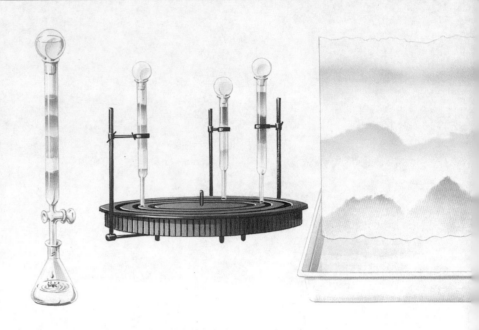

Chemical Analysis

Finding out what is in chemical substances, and how much, is called chemical analysis. One important method for analysing mixtures is chromatography, invented in 1903 by a Russian chemist, M.S. Tswett, for separating and identifying the coloured pigments of plant leaves.

From the 1930s, a method called paper chromatography was used to analyse many more chemical substances, including dyestuffs, vitamins, fats, and blood pigments. A drop of liquid containing the substance to be analysed is placed at the bottom of a sheet of porous paper. The different parts or components of the mixture then creep up the paper at different rates, so that they separate out from one another. An even more recent invention is the gas chromatograph, which can analyse an even wider range of substances.

Spectrochemical analysis is another powerful method of identifying what a substance contains. It has a history going all the way back to Isaac Newton's discovery of the spectrum (see pages 30-31). Newton discovered that white light can be split up by a glass prism into a number of coloured bands. In a similar

way, the light from every chemical element, when this is made white-hot, will separate out into bands which identify that element.

In 1859 an instrument called the spectroscope was invented for this purpose by two Germans, Gustav Kirchhoff (1824-1887) and Robert Bunsen (1811-1899). Spectroscopes are not only used in the chemical laboratory. In astronomy, they analyse the light coming from stars and other parts of outer space, telling us what chemical elements and compounds exist there.

Lasers and Fibre Optics

A laser is an instrument that produces an intense beam of coherent light, that is, light of a single wavelength, where all the waves are "in step". (By contrast, light from an ordinary electric bulb is of many wavelengths, not in step.) The first working laser was built in 1960 by the inventor Theodore Maiman in the USA.

Lasers have an increasing number of applications. Their intense beams of light extend a very long way, so that they can be used for signalling. More frivolously, criss-crossing beams of laser light are sometimes used to make spectacular, brightly-

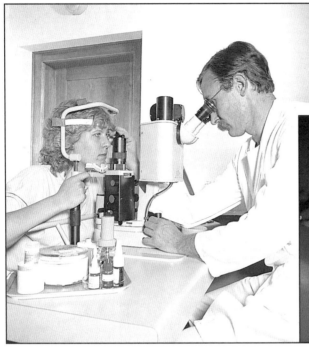

Left and below: Versatile lasers: their high-energy light beams are used for such widely different purposes as welding back a detached retina in the human eye and cutting out complex shapes from a steel sheet.

coloured displays against the night sky.

The concentrated energy of laser beams can also take the form of heat. This leads to such different applications as welding back the retina of the human eye after it has become detached, and use in weapons designed to explode enemy missiles during war in space or "Star Wars". A laser is also part of the compact disc recorder (see pages 108-109).

Fibre optics also uses light waves. It employs long glass fibres, each composed of two different layers of glass. Light shone in one end of these fibres passes mainly *along* the fibres, because the outer layer of glass refracts the light waves in to the inner layer of glass. Very little light escapes sideways.

Fibre-optics instruments contain ropes or bundles of these lighted-up fibres, which allow someone looking down one end to see what is happening at the other. A surgeon may use such an instrument to look inside a patient's body, and even carry out internal operations without the need to open the patient up.

Messages can also be sent along optic fibres, and fibre-optic cables now span both the Atlantic and Pacific Oceans.

Right: A fibre optics cable contains thousands of long glass fibres, along which light passes. One use of fibre optics is to send picture messages.

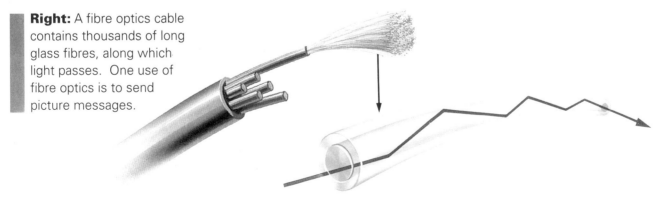

COMPUTERS

People have always looked for quick ways to work out sums and have invented machines for doing so. One of the oldest calculating machines is the abacus, on which the answers to sums are found by moving beads on rods or wires.

Thousands of years later than the abacus, further calculating machines were invented, the latest of which are the computers we use today. To "compute" a sum means the same as to "calculate" it.

Analogue and Digital Computers

There are two basic types of computer or calculator. One type is called digital, because such machines work directly with numbers, or digits. Both the ancient abacus and the modern desk computer are examples of digital computers.

The other type is called analogue, because these machines do not work directly with numbers but with some other quantity that varies and can be measured: an analogous quantity. One example of an analogue computer is the slide rule, invented by an Englishman, John Gunter, in 1620. This employs lengths as the analogue to numbers. Other, more complicated analogue computers are used in industry for measuring and controlling processes such as the rate of flow of a product in a factory.

Early digital computers, or calculators, were mechanical machines using interlocking toothed wheels. One wheel would rotate ten times to turn another once, and by such means simple arithmetical sums could be quickly performed. The French philosopher Blaise Pascal (1623-1660) invented a calculating machine of this sort in 1642, which was used for gambling calculations.

In the 1820s an Englishman, Charles Babbage (1792-1871), invented a mechanical calculating machine that would carry out even more complicated arithmetic. He went on to design still more advanced machines, but none of these "difference engines" was completed.

Modern Computers

The "father" of today's computers may be said to be Alan Turing (1912-1954), an English mathematician who invented a theoretical digital computer in 1937. In 1944, the first such computer was built in the USA by Howard Aiken. Named the Harvard Mark 1, it was more than 15 m in length and filled a large room.

Equally large but more powerful was a computer built in 1946 by J.G. Brainerd and others at the University of Pennsylvania, USA. This was the first truly electronic computer. It employed vacuum tubes or radio valves (see pages 108-109) and could multiply 300 numbers each second. It printed out its answers on punched cards, a system invented in 1890 by Herman Hollerith in the USA.

The next major advance in computing was the replacement of bulky radio valves by much smaller

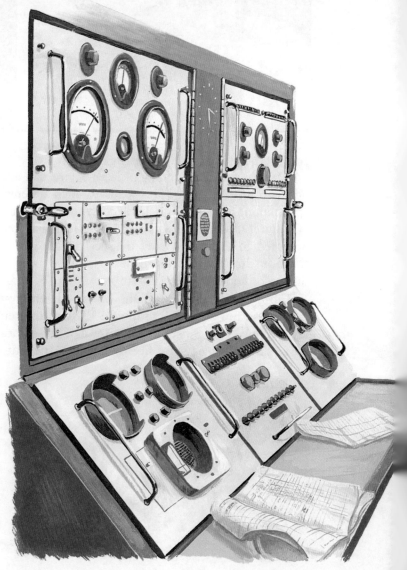

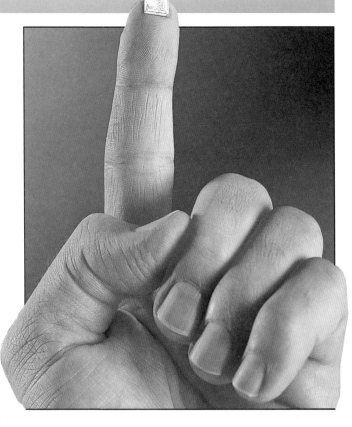

transistors. The transistor was invented in 1945 by William Shockley, John Bardeen and others in the USA. In another advance, electronic printers replaced the older punched card printers.

Computers were shrunk even further by printed circuits, developed after 1945. All electrical wiring was replaced by tiny electrical circuits deposited or printed on non-conducting boards. In 1958 computers were shrunk yet again, when the first integrated circuit was invented. Integrated circuits are single chips of a hard non-metal, silicon, on which highly complicated electrical circuits are micro-miniaturized. A microchip of today, less than 4 mm square, may contain millions of transistors.

Below: An early electronic computer of the 1950s filled a whole room. Today, even a pocket calculator is more powerful!

Above: The tiny but powerful silicon chip which is used in computers of today.

Below: Computing can be carried out almost anywhere, using a laptop or desktop machine.

PRINTED CIRCUITS INVENTED 1945 • INTEGRATED CIRCUITS 1958

121

SPACECRAFT

ROCKET POWER

If you blow up a balloon, then let it go, it flies wildly around the room. This is caused by reaction to the thrust of the air rushing out of the balloon's neck. A rocket works in just the same way, and it was by developing rocket power that artificial Satellites became a practical proposition.

In a rocket engine, propellants, called fuel, and an oxidizer (which supplies the oxygen to burn the fuel), are ignited (set on fire) to form hot gases (exhaust) which are forced through a nozzle at the end of the engine. It is this thrust that propels the rocket. Unlike the balloon, the rocket's flight path is controlled by gyroscopes and computer guidance systems to make sure it keeps heading in the right direction.

Most modern rockets use liquid fuel, such as kerosene (paraffin) or liquid hydrogen, which is burned with liquid oxygen to produce the combustion and thrust. Liquid hydrogen fuel and liquid oxygen oxidizer are called cryogenic propellants because they are gases that have been cooled so much that they have turned into a liquid. The propellants are pumped from storage tanks into a chamber where they are mixed and ignited. Some propellants, such as hydrazine and nitric oxide, are called hypergolic because they ignite as soon as they come into contact, in an explosive chemical reaction.

The Space Shuttle is unusual in that it uses both liquid and solid propellants. The three main engines on the Shuttle itself use liquid oxygen and liquid hydrogen, while the two big white booster rockets either side of it are propelled by a solid propellant, which is a mix of chemicals in a kind of rubbery substance.

The Multi-Stage Rocket

To carry an artificial satellite into orbit, a rocket must reach a speed of about 28,800 km/h so it is fast enough to overcome the pull of the Earth's gravity. One rocket cannot do this on its own, so several fuel tanks are joined together; each section is called a stage. The stages are stacked one on top of the other or added at the side of the rocket. Most space rockets have three stages, each one igniting in turn to increase the speed gradually; they separate and fall away as the fuel runs out; this makes the rocket much lighter.

The Space Shuttle has a large tank which holds the fuel for its engines and two solid-fuel rocket boosters

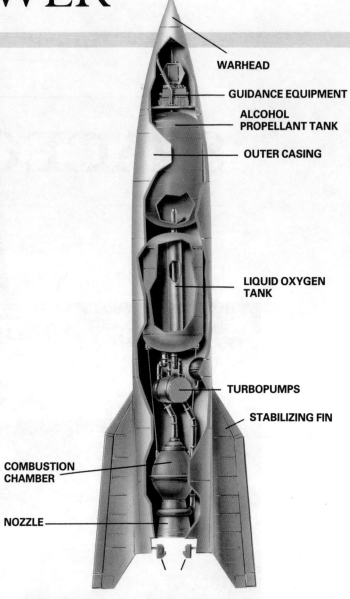

WARHEAD

GUIDANCE EQUIPMENT

ALCOHOL PROPELLANT TANK

OUTER CASING

LIQUID OXYGEN TANK

TURBOPUMPS

STABILIZING FIN

COMBUSTION CHAMBER

NOZZLE

Above: One of the first large rockets was the German V2, which was used as a weapon during World War II.

are strapped to the sides of the fuel tank. These give an extra boost during the first two minutes of flight and then parachute back to Earth to be used again. The liquid propellant engines burn for another six minutes before the Shuttle reaches orbit, then the empty fuel tank falls away and breaks up. Smaller rockets on the Shuttle itself are sometimes needed for the final boost to the planned orbit.

GODDARD BUILT AND FIRED FIRST LIQUID-FUELLED ROCKET ON 16 MARCH 1926

Right: The world's tallest rocket, the American Saturn V. Standing 111 m tall, it weighed 3,000 t on the launch pad. The three-stage Saturn V launched the Apollo crews to the Moon between 1969 and 1972.

THIRD STAGE FIRES TO THRUST THE APOLLO SPACECRAFT INTO ORBIT THEN SEPARATES

SECOND STAGE FIRES, BOOSTS THE APOLLO SPACECRAFT HIGHER AND FASTER, THEN SEPARATES

STAGE SEPARATION SKIRT

Left: The staging sequence of Saturn V with a first stage thrust of 3.5 million kg. Earth orbit is reached 11 mins after blast off from the Kennedy Space Center, Florida.

FIRST STAGE BURNS OUT AND FALLS AWAY

SATURN V, WORLD'S MOST POWERFUL ROCKET, 111 M TALL, CARRIED 3,000 T OF FUEL

SATELLITES

SCIENTIFIC SATELLITE

SATELLITE DESIGN

Because satellites only travel in space, they need not be streamlined, but can be whatever shape is best for the job they have to do. The body of a satellite is usually made of ultra-lightweight aluminium alloys and strong plastics. On it are all kinds of equipment, such as cameras, telescopes, detectors and many different measuring instruments which stick out into space. Telstar (left) was the first communications satellite, launched in 1962.

Artificial satellites are the most common kind of spacecraft and they stay in space for many years. They have a variety of uses: communications, astronomy and observation of the Earth and its atmosphere from space.

A satellite reaches orbit when it is travelling at a speed that is fast enough to overcome the force of the Earth's gravity, which is trying to pull it back to Earth, while at the same time, it is not fast enough to make the satellite speed away from Earth's gravity altogether.

About 5,000 artificial satellites have been launched into Earth orbit since Sputnik 1 in 1957. They were not, however, all sent into the same orbit. In a typical orbit, the craft will travel around the Earth at about 400 km altitude. At this height, it will be travelling at about 28,800 km/h in a circular orbit. If the satellite is in a much higher orbit, its speed need not be as great because the Earth's gravity becomes weaker.

Most satellites are sent into elliptical orbits which have a high point (apogee) and a low point (perigee) above the Earth.

Different Orbits

Satellites go into orbits which travel around the Earth in different directions. For example, a Space Shuttle may orbit so that it crosses the equator at an angle of 28°. This is called the orbital inclination. It means that during its orbits, the Shuttle never reaches further north or south of the 28° latitude on the Earth. A satellite that orbits at 90°, however, flies over the poles of the Earth and therefore covers all latitudes. If it travels in a low orbit around the poles, it takes 90 minutes to go around once, and in one day it makes 17 orbits while the Earth has rotated once, so the satellite flies over every area of the Earth in this period. This is an important orbit for some observation satellites, particularly those that spy!

Another very important orbit is called the geostationary orbit. Here the satellite enters a circular orbit at an altitude of about 36,000 km where it takes 24 hours to make one orbit, which is the same time it takes the Earth to rotate on its axis. The satellite also orbits at 0° inclination, directly above the equator, so it seems to be stationary, hovering over the same spot on the Earth. This is the perfect situation for a communications satellite which is rather like a TV and radio aerial in the sky.

IN A CIRCULAR ORBIT OF 400 KM, SATELLITES TAKE 90 MINUTES TO CIRCLE EARTH

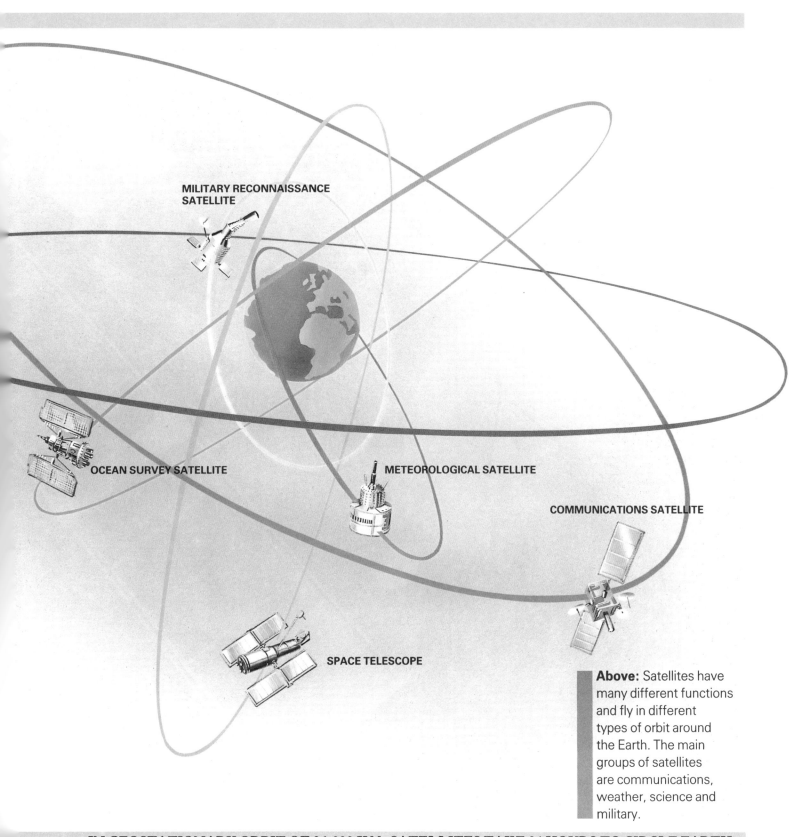

MILITARY RECONNAISSANCE SATELLITE

OCEAN SURVEY SATELLITE

METEOROLOGICAL SATELLITE

COMMUNICATIONS SATELLITE

SPACE TELESCOPE

Above: Satellites have many different functions and fly in different types of orbit around the Earth. The main groups of satellites are communications, weather, science and military.

IN GEOSTATIONARY ORBIT OF 36,000 KM, SATELLITES TAKE 24 HOURS TO CIRCLE EARTH

127

POWER FOR SPACECRAFT

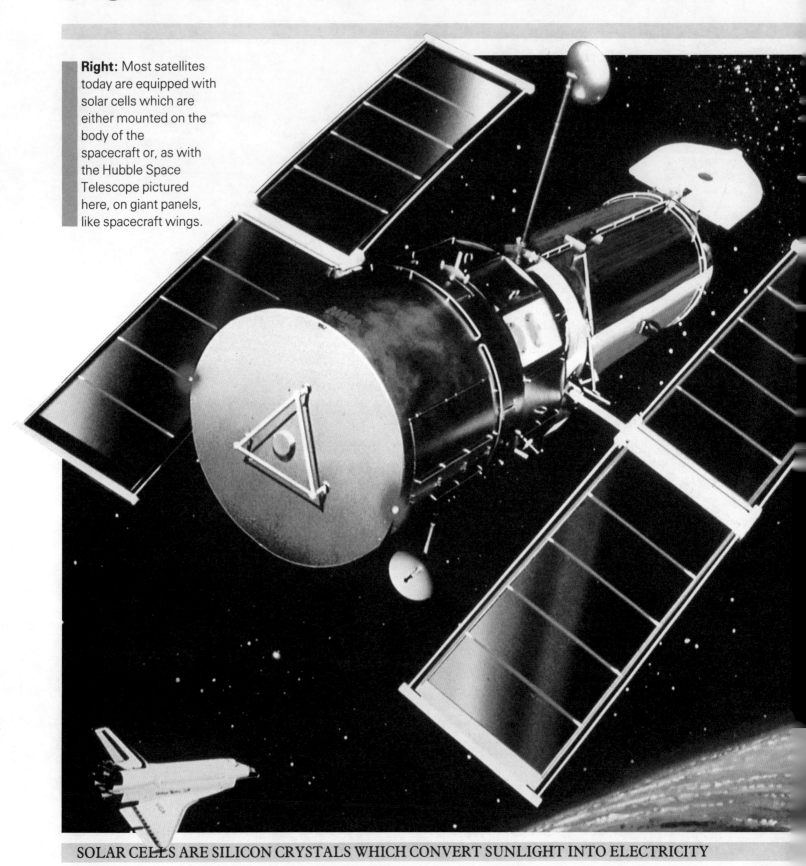

Right: Most satellites today are equipped with solar cells which are either mounted on the body of the spacecraft or, as with the Hubble Space Telescope pictured here, on giant panels, like spacecraft wings.

SOLAR CELLS ARE SILICON CRYSTALS WHICH CONVERT SUNLIGHT INTO ELECTRICITY

The first artificial Earth satellite, Sputnik 1, was powered by a chemical battery. However, after a few days the battery ran out of power and the satellite's radio transmitter went dead. In 1958, America launched the satellite Vanguard 1 which tested a new type of system powered by solar cells. These are tiny pieces of silicon glass that absorb the Sun's light and convert this energy into electrical power.

Solar Energy

Thousands of solar cells mounted on spacecraft can provide 1,500 watts of electricity or even more. Most satellites today are powered this way. Some satellites have giant wings and the solar cells are mounted on these solar panels. Other satellites have their whole body covered with solar cells. Scientists are studying the use of more productive solar cell materials, such as gallium arsenide crystals.

Fuel Cells

There are other types of electrical generators on spacecraft. The Space Shuttle uses fuel cells. These are provided with oxygen and hydrogen propellants from liquid gas tanks on the Shuttle. The cells then convert the chemical energy of the reaction between the two gases into electrical energy. A by-product of this fuel cell process is drinkable water.

Radioactive Power

Some satellites which need very large amounts of electricity, such as spacecraft using large radar scanners to observe the Earth in great detail, use radioactive power sources. These spacecraft have a radioactive fuel core of uranium or plutonium. As the radioactive material decays, it produces energy which is then converted to electricity. Spacecraft that travel into the distant Solar System where there is no sunlight to power solar cells use this radioactive fuel system, called a radioisotope thermoelectric generator or RTG. The Voyager 2 spacecraft, which was launched in 1977 and travelled to Jupiter, Saturn, Uranus and Neptune, reaching Neptune in 1989, could not have operated had it not been for its plutonium-powered RTG.

The USA has plans to power space stations of the future with huge solar mirrors. These concentrate the Sun's heat and use this heat, or thermal energy, to drive generators which provide electricity.

SPACEPROBES TRAVELLING INTO DEEP SPACE ARE POWERED BY NUCLEAR BATTERIES

COMSATS

TV SIGNALS FROM AN OUTSIDE BROADCAST TRUCK
TRAVEL BY CABLE TO A MOBILE RECEIVER,
WHICH TRANSMITS THE SIGNALS
TO A COMMUNICATIONS SATELLITE

Above: Communications satellites are used to relay TV direct to homes; transmit telephone, telex, fax and computer data; and to keep mobile vehicles in touch with headquarters.

TELSTAR WAS FIRST COMMUNICATIONS SATELLITE, LAUNCHED BY USA IN 1962

130

In 1962, the USA launched the world's first communications satellite, called Telstar. It could receive television pictures and relay them live across the Atlantic Ocean. This meant that when an American astronaut called Walter Schirra was launched into the Earth's orbit aboard Mercury 8 later that year, TV viewers in Britain were able to see his launch the same day via the Telstar communications satellite. Before this, a film of the event would have been sent by plane, so that it could not have been seen until the next day. Today, most long-distance communications: TV, telephone, telex, fax (facsimile transmission) and computer data go through communications satellites, or comsats.

An international organization called INTELSAT (International Telecommunications Satellite Organization) was set up in 1964 to provide worldwide communications for commercial use. Today there are over 100 member countries and they own and operate the world's largest and most powerful commercial communications satellite called Intelsat 6. The first satellite in the Intelsat 6 series was launched in 1989. Intelsat 6 is shaped like a dustbin, is 12 m high and has several dishes attached to its top. These are the communications antennae. In its stationary orbit, 36,000 km above the equator, Intelsat 6 relays 30,000 simultaneous telephone calls between two continents, operates three television relay channels at the same time and transmits 3 billion bits of computer information per second.

How a Communications Satellite Works

A communications satellite collects electronic information – such as voice, data and TV pictures – from a transmitting station on the ground, increases the power of these signals by amplifying them, then retransmits the signals to ground stations on Earth. The TV satellites which provide programmes directly to homes equipped with small satellite dishes operate on very high power, enabling the signal to be collected by small receivers.

Communications satellites need a lot of electricity to operate. Intelsat 6, for example, requires 2,400 watts of power and this power is provided by solar cells mounted around its enormous cylindrical body.

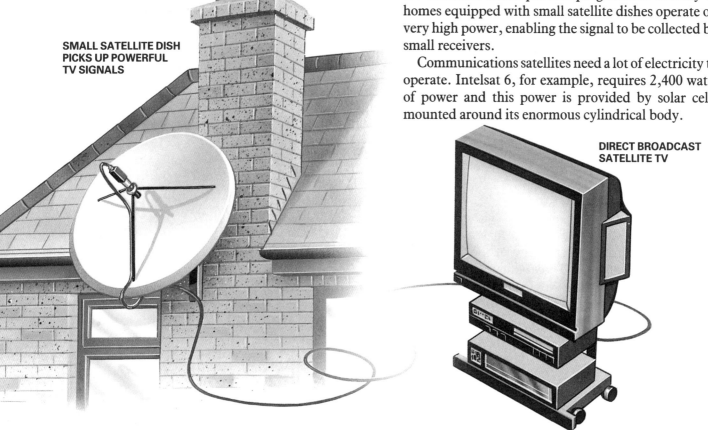

SMALL SATELLITE DISH PICKS UP POWERFUL TV SIGNALS

DIRECT BROADCAST SATELLITE TV

INTELSAT 6, 12 M LONG, CAN HANDLE 30,000 TWO-WAY CALLS AT THE SAME TIME

WATCHING THE EARTH

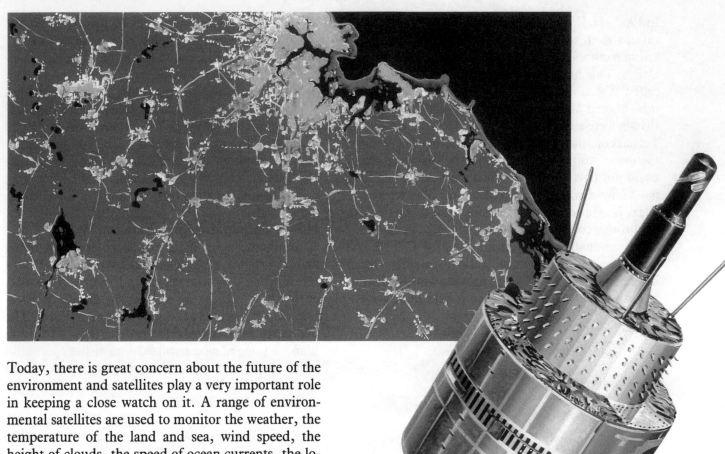

Today, there is great concern about the future of the environment and satellites play a very important role in keeping a close watch on it. A range of environmental satellites are used to monitor the weather, the temperature of the land and sea, wind speed, the height of clouds, the speed of ocean currents, the location of minerals and water on land, the movement of animals, industrial pollution, deforestation of the jungles, and even the hole in the ozone layer of the Earth's atmosphere.

Environmental Satellites in Orbit

There are two types of environmental satellite. A satellite in a stationary orbit 36,000 km above the Earth returns images of one third of the face of the Earth every few minutes. Three of these satellites strategically located at points over the equator can therefore observe the whole Earth. A polar orbiting satellite covers the whole globe in a day from a low orbit (about 800 km above the Earth), orbiting 17 times in one day, as the Earth rotates beneath it. Many of these satellites also carry receivers which can pick up distress signals from people lost at sea or on land.

The Work of Environmental Satellites

Environmental satellites are fitted with many types of instruments to monitor aspects of the environment

Top: A false colour image from the US spacecraft, Landsat 5, showing the city of Boston. The red colour is lush vegetation.

Above: Meteosat, a European weather satellite which is in geostationary orbit around the Earth.

ENVIRONMENTAL SATELLITES MONITOR THE EARTH'S ATMOSPHERE AND SURFACE

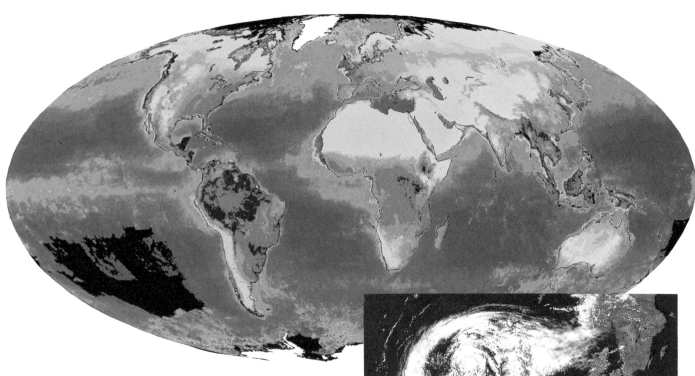

Above: An image of the Earth's vegetation showing details such as the level of plankton (microscopic plants) in the sea (red and yellow) and the rain forests (light green).

Right: Europe as seen from the US weather satellite NOAA 9, which orbits around the Earth's poles. A severe storm system covers most of the British Isles.

and can often spot the hidden details. Some send back photographs which show the Earth as we would see it, but photographs are also taken with infra-red cameras. These can "see" through cloud and detect infra-red (heat) radiation, so the images show how hot or cold parts of the sea or land are.

Other instruments identify chemicals in the atmosphere; these are used to monitor pollution, the greenhouse effect and the hole in the ozone layer. Images of oil slicks and industrial waste polluting the water can also be produced.

Some imaging systems use radar waves to make up pictures of the Earth, particularly to map the surface of the Earth under the sea. Photographs taken by satellites have even been used to help geologists find rare minerals in remote parts of the world. Radar pictures have also taken a peep into history: Space Shuttle images showed the remains of a civilization under the sand in Africa.

TIROS 1, LAUNCHED BY THE USA IN APRIL 1960, WAS THE FIRST WEATHER SATELLITE

MILITARY SATELLITES

Over half the satellites sent into Earth orbit by the USA and others are used for military purposes: to observe enemy territory. Some take close-up photographs of targets on the ground, while other satellites are used for eavesdropping on radio communications and defence radars. Some military satellites have more specialized purposes, such as monitoring enemy launch sites to give early warnings of missile attack, or use radar and other sensors to track enemy ships and submarines. There are also military communications satellites which are used to link the leader of a country with a troop commander in the battlefield.

The first military satellites were called Discoverer and were launched by the USA 30 years ago. These small capsules held cameras which took photographs of locations on the ground. The capsules returned to Earth and were caught in mid-air by aircraft trailing a snare-net, rather like a fishing net. The film was processed and the photographs analyzed.

Today, such recoverable spacecraft are still used. They use camera systems that are powerful enough to locate an object on Earth about 3 m wide from an orbit about 300 km high. The main disadvantage of these spacecraft is that the film has to be recovered and processed, and this can take valuable time.

Modern Spy Satellites

Spy satellites have been developed which electronically scan the ground from orbit and transmit the images to Earth by radio. These can now return images with as good a clarity, or resolution, as film cameras. They are also able to maintain a continuous watch without running out of film.

Electronic monitoring, or elint, satellites carry huge dish aerials which pick up all sorts of radio transmissions. This radio jumble of noise can then be transmitted to a ground station and filtered, so that important and perhaps secret conversations can be bugged.

Other military satellites are used to monitor the weather for naval, air and land operations and others are used to maintain secret communications. Communications are so good today that a soldier with a small radio back-pack can talk via satellite with headquarters on the other side of the world. Similar, small satellite receivers enable soldiers, naval commanders and pilots to navigate with extreme precision, using several navigation satellites.

STAR WARS

In 1983, US President Reagan announced his Strategic Defence Initiative or Star Wars plan to put high energy lasers into orbit to shoot down incoming enemy missiles. The results of this research (left): a Titan missile stage is destroyed by a chemical laser in a test at White Sands, New Mexico. The test was to see how vulnerable a liquid-fuelled rocket is to an attack. The rocket stage was stressed to simulate exact flight conditions.

WITH MILITARY SATELLITES, USA AND RUSSIA KNOW THE ARMAMENTS EACH SIDE HAS

Above: Cape Canaveral is the triangular sand spit at the bottom of this photograph taken from the Space Shuttle. The Kennedy Space Center is above right, where the Shuttle runway and two launch pads can be seen.

Left: A Delta booster is launched from Cape Canaveral carrying a Star Wars experiment into orbit. Several Star Wars tests are planned before the system is in place.

FIRST US MILITARY SATELLITES, CALLED DISCOVERER, WERE LAUNCHED IN 1959

SPACE TRAVEL

THE SPACE RACE

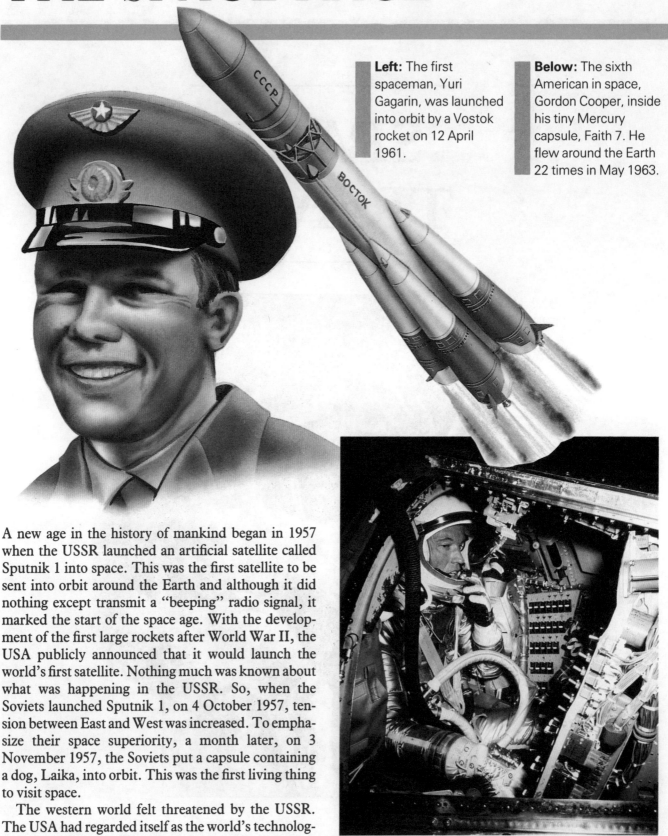

Left: The first spaceman, Yuri Gagarin, was launched into orbit by a Vostok rocket on 12 April 1961.

Below: The sixth American in space, Gordon Cooper, inside his tiny Mercury capsule, Faith 7. He flew around the Earth 22 times in May 1963.

A new age in the history of mankind began in 1957 when the USSR launched an artificial satellite called Sputnik 1 into space. This was the first satellite to be sent into orbit around the Earth and although it did nothing except transmit a "beeping" radio signal, it marked the start of the space age. With the development of the first large rockets after World War II, the USA publicly announced that it would launch the world's first satellite. Nothing much was known about what was happening in the USSR. So, when the Soviets launched Sputnik 1, on 4 October 1957, tension between East and West was increased. To emphasize their space superiority, a month later, on 3 November 1957, the Soviets put a capsule containing a dog, Laika, into orbit. This was the first living thing to visit space.

The western world felt threatened by the USSR. The USA had regarded itself as the world's technolog-

ical leader and now found itself outpaced by the Soviet leap into space. Top priorities were given to space activities. America's first attempt to place a satellite into orbit failed when the rocket blew up on the launch pad. It was not until January 1958 that Jupiter C launched the first US satellite Explorer I into orbit. The Soviets continued to send up Sputniks and new Luniks. Luna 2 was the first spacecraft to reach the Moon in 1959 and Luna 3 was the first satellite to photograph the far side of the Moon.

America suffered many failures, which were seen all over the world because of the open nature of its programme. The USSR suffered failures, too, but the news never leaked out, so it formed an invincible lead in what had become the space race.

In August 1960, the Soviets sent dogs into orbit for one day to test the new Vostok spacecraft in which Soviet cosmonauts would eventually fly; it was disguised under the name Sputnik 5. The two dogs, Belka and Strelka, were the first living things to return from orbit.

The First Men in Space

The next step was to launch the first man in space. On 12 April 1961, Yuri Alekseyevich Gagarin was rocketed into space and, after completing one orbit, the automatic controls of his spacecraft brought him safely back to Earth. The first American was sent into space on 5 May 1961, when Alan Shepherd made a simple up-and-down sub-orbital flight in a Mercury capsule. The first American to orbit Earth was John Glenn in 1962. The Soviets launched a new spacecraft and, in March 1965, Alexei Leonov crawled through the airlock of Voskhod 2 to make the first walk in space.

The Moon Race

In 1961, President Kennedy had set the USA the target of landing a man on the Moon by 1970 – before the USSR. Project Gemini in the mid-1960s pioneered most of the systems that would be needed for the trip to the Moon in the Apollo spacecraft. Space-walking (to perform tasks outside the capsule in space), rendezvous and docking of spacecraft, manoeuvring in space and spending enough time in space (14 days) for the lunar trip were all tried out on the 12 Gemini missions.

Above: Ed White was the first American to walk in space on 3 June 1965. A cable connected him to Gemini 4 and supplied him with oxygen.

The Apollo project was the final stage of the US programme to place a man on the Moon and bring him back safely to Earth. After a number of test flights, first around the Earth and then around the Moon without landing, a giant Saturn V rocket lifted Apollo 11 from Cape Canaveral in Florida on 16 July 1969. On 21 July, Neil Armstrong stepped onto the surface of the Moon.

MAN ON THE MOON

On 21 July 1969, Neil Armstrong climbed down the ladder of the lunar lander and onto the surface of the Moon. Placing his foot on the lunar soil, he said, "That's one small step for man, one giant leap for mankind." He was the first person to set foot on the Moon. Buzz Aldrin then joined Armstrong on the Moon's surface. They spent over two hours doing experiments and collected over 20 kg of rock and soil. Then they returned to the spacecraft and blasted off to rejoin the third astronaut, Michael Collins, who had remained orbiting the Moon while they visited it.

The Apollo Spacecraft

Armstrong, Aldrin and Collins had travelled to the Moon aboard Apollo 11. This was shot into space by the most powerful rocket ever built, Saturn V. The Apollo spacecraft consisted of three parts. The command module was a three-man pressurized capsule where the astronauts sat for take-off; it was also the only part of the spaceship to return to Earth. This was attached to the service module which contained fuel

Below: Apollo landings. 11: July 1969, Sea of Tranquillity. 12: November 1969, Ocean of Storms. 14: February 1971, Fra Mauro. 15: July 1971, Hadley Rille. 16: April 1972, Descartes. 17: December 1972, Taurus Littrow.

Above: An Apollo lunar module on the Moon.

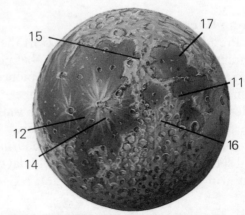

LIFT-OFF 9.32 AM WEDNESDAY 16 JULY 1969 • MAN ON MOON 2.30 AM MONDAY 21 JULY

and equipment, plus a rocket motor used to correct the course when travelling to and from the Moon. The third part of the Apollo spacecraft was the lunar module which went down to the Moon's surface. The lunar module was abandoned before the flight home and the service module was thrown away just before the command module entered the Earth's atmosphere, making the Apollo programme very expensive. It is estimated to have cost $25,000 million.

There were other manned expeditions to the Moon after Apollo 11. However, one mission, Apollo 13, went wrong. An oxygen tank exploded on the way to the Moon, so the landing was cancelled, but luckily none of the astronauts was injured.

Exploring the Moon

Between December 1968 and December 1972, 23 people went to the Moon and 12 walked on the surface. During the Apollo 11, 12, 14, 15, 16 and 17 missions, 160 hours were spent exploring the surface at six different sites; they covered 100 km. Apollo 15, 16 and 17 carried the lunar roving vehicle or Moon buggy. This small, four-wheeled car was powered by electric motor and had a maximum speed of 16 km/h. The astronauts collected 2,196 samples of the Moon, weighing a total of 385 kg, for analysis. They carried out experiments and set up scientific stations, one of which is still sending information back to Earth. They also took over 30,000 photographs.

Below: Apollo 15 commander Dave Scott salutes the US flag at Hadley Base.

12 APOLLO ASTRONAUTS LAND ON MOON BETWEEN JULY 1969 AND DECEMBER 1972

THE SPACE SHUTTLE

Nobody throws away an airliner after just one flight, so why throw away a rocket and a spacecraft? This was the logic behind the development of the Space Shuttle. In 1972, the USA decided to build such a shuttle. It would be in service in 1978 and be capable of making over 50 trips a year, making space travel almost as routine as airflight.

The first Space Shuttle went into space on 12 April 1981. The main part of the Space Shuttle is the orbiter which looks like an ordinary aeroplane. It is launched like a rocket but flies back to land on a runway like an aircraft. The orbiter measures 37.2 m long and has a wingspan of 23.8 m. The forward compartment carries up to eight people, including scientists who carry out experiments in space. This is the only pressurized section of the orbiter. The upper flight deck looks very like that of an aeroplane only with more dials, controls and instruments and at the rear of the upper deck are controls for launching satellites. The lower deck consists of a galley or kitchen, toilet and sleeping quarters. Most of the orbiter's length is taken up by the huge payload bay which can carry a payload (cargo) of 29 t into orbit and bring 14.5 t back to Earth. Inside the payload bay is a remote-controlled arm used for handling satellites. At the rear of the orbiter are the three main engines used during launch; in space the Shuttle manoeuvres using small rockets in the nose and tail.

The Space Shuttle is a remarkable flying machine. It is flown by five computers. Four are used to fly the Shuttle at any one time, with their decisions crosschecked to spot any errors. Using the Shuttle, it has been possible to fly up to a faulty satellite and repair it, or bring it back to Earth. It can carry three satellites at once and place them into orbit from its payload bay. However, the Space Shuttle is not entirely reusable; it jettisons its empty 33-t fuel tank which burns up in the atmosphere just before it goes into orbit. Nor is it as safe or reliable as an airliner. In January 1986, the Space Shuttle exploded just after it was launched, killing seven astronauts and completely destroying the Shuttle. Only about ten launches a year are possible, not the 50 first hoped.

The Future of the Shuttle

In the future, the Space Shuttle will be used to carry parts of an international space station, called Freedom, into orbit, where Shuttle crews will assemble the space station helped by mechanical robot arms. The Shuttle will then be used to fly crews and equipment to operate the space station. The Shuttle will also be used to place huge telescopes into orbit which can be serviced by later Shuttle crews.

The US Shuttle is just the first of several that have been planned. Later versions may be launched by more powerful rockets and will therefore be able to carry more equipment. Eventually, an entirely new version, called Shuttle 2, may be built using new engines and materials technology to reduce the cost of going to and from space.

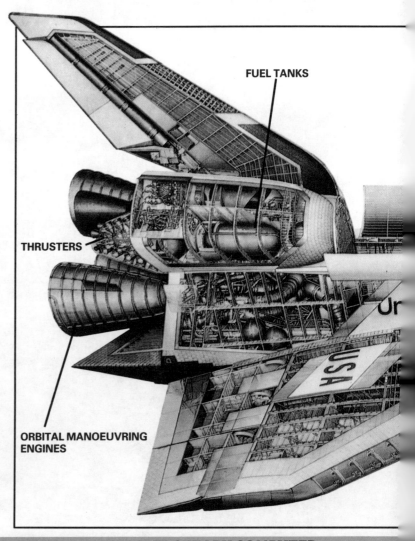

FUEL TANKS

THRUSTERS

ORBITAL MANOEUVRING ENGINES

USA

ORBITER 37.2 M LONG, WINGSPAN OF 23.8 M, WEIGHT 68,000 KG, FLOWN BY COMPUTER

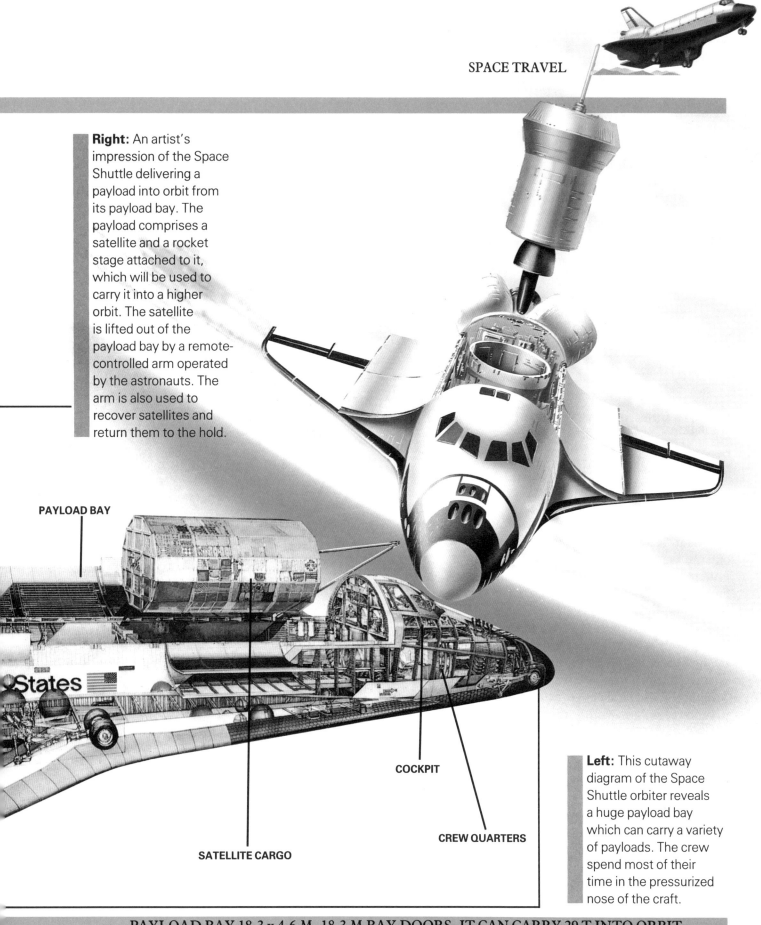

Right: An artist's impression of the Space Shuttle delivering a payload into orbit from its payload bay. The payload comprises a satellite and a rocket stage attached to it, which will be used to carry it into a higher orbit. The satellite is lifted out of the payload bay by a remote-controlled arm operated by the astronauts. The arm is also used to recover satellites and return them to the hold.

PAYLOAD BAY

COCKPIT

CREW QUARTERS

SATELLITE CARGO

Left: This cutaway diagram of the Space Shuttle orbiter reveals a huge payload bay which can carry a variety of payloads. The crew spend most of their time in the pressurized nose of the craft.

PAYLOAD BAY 18.3 x 4.6 M, 18.3 M BAY DOORS, IT CAN CARRY 29 T INTO ORBIT

DANGERS OF SPACE

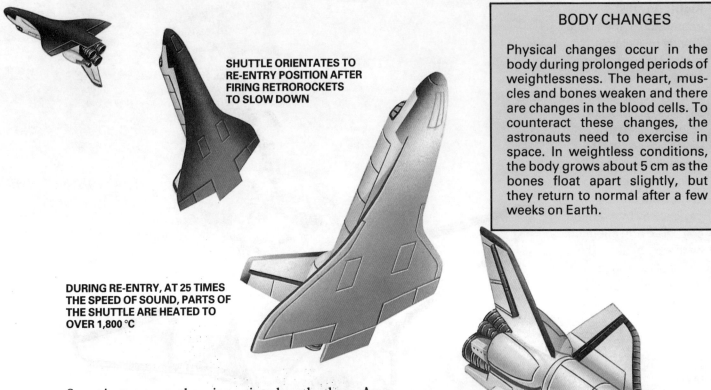

SHUTTLE ORIENTATES TO RE-ENTRY POSITION AFTER FIRING RETROROCKETS TO SLOW DOWN

DURING RE-ENTRY, AT 25 TIMES THE SPEED OF SOUND, PARTS OF THE SHUTTLE ARE HEATED TO OVER 1,800 °C

THE SHUTTLE IS A GLIDER DESCENDING SEVEN TIMES STEEPER AND 20 TIMES FASTER THAN AN AIRLINER

Space is a vacuum, there is no air to breathe there. An astronaut needs a pressurized cockpit and, to work outside the spacecraft, a spacesuit. Astronauts also need to be protected from the intense heat of the sunlight and the intense cold of the darkness in space.

Van Allen Belts

The Earth is surrounded by two radiation belts. These are made up of atomic particles from the Sun, trapped by the Earth's magnetic field. Called Van Allen belts after the scientist who discovered them, they lie about 3,000 and 22,000 km above the Earth. It is dangerous to venture for long at altitudes in which these radiation belts exist.

Space Pollution

Man has started to pollute space, creating a new kind of hazard as millions of man-made objects orbit the Earth in every direction. This debris ranges from flakes of paint and insulation shed by spacecraft to discarded satellites which no longer work and the rocket stages used to launch them. A flake of paint travelling in the opposite direction to a Space Shuttle, with a closing speed of 57,000 km/h, could smash the window, depressurizing the craft and killing the crew.

Above: The Shuttle lands like an airliner after entry into the Earth's atmosphere. Friction heats the Shuttle to over 1,800 °C so the aluminium structure is protected by special heatshield tiles, the nose cap and leading edges of the wings by an extremely strong carbon material.

PART OF SKYLAB 2 X 1 M FELL TO AUSTRALIA • 10 KG PIECE OF SPUTNIK FELL TO USA

Space Travel

Getting into and out of space is dangerous. The rocket can blow up during launch when the propellants are ignited. As the launch rocket accelerates, the astronauts suffer a tremendous gravitational pull on their bodies. These g-forces make them feel very heavy. Once in space, the astronauts become weightless and float inside the spacecraft. Without strenuous exercise and careful health checks, long journeys in weightless conditions can be dangerous because the body has to withstand the strain of returning to gravity. On re-entering the Earth's atmosphere, g-forces again pull on the body, then, after the spacecraft lands, Earth's continuous one-g gravity can have detrimental effects on a body that has been used to weightlessness for very long periods.

The re-entry itself is very hazardous. Travelling at 30,000 km/h, the spacecraft is heated up as it plunges into the outer layers of the Earth's atmosphere. Friction with the air causes the spacecraft to glow and, without a heatshield, it would burn up. Fortunately, there has never been a heatshield failure on a manned spaceflight – yet.

Right: A US Shuttle astronaut wears a spacesuit with a portable life support system backpack to work outside the craft.

LANDING AT 400 KM/H

SPACE SHUTTLE RE-ENTERS ATMOSPHERE AT 30,000 KM/H, HEATED TO OVER 1,800 °C

SPACE STATIONS

In science fiction books and films, space stations are usually crewed by hundreds of people living in a self-supporting environment. The reality is very different. Space stations are orbiting spacecraft in which a few astronauts stay for weeks or months at a time to carry out scientific experiments.

US Space Stations

In 1973, the Americans launched a space station called Skylab. This huge craft consisted of the top stage of a Saturn V rocket which was converted to carry American crews of three at a time. Skylab contained equipment for carrying out scientific experiments, such as processing materials, and observing the Earth and Sun. The astronauts also carried out medical experiments on themselves to study the effects of prolonged spaceflight on the human body.

The Skylab project finished in 1974 but, since then, America has not launched another station. There are plans for a new space station called Freedom to be built in the 1990s but these are threatened with budget cuts. If Freedom is built, it will consist of several pressurized, cylindrical modules providing living quarters and laboratories, joined together and mounted on a giant girder. The space station will be equipped with large solar panels to provide electricity.

Soviet Space Stations

The USSR took the lead in space station flights. Soviet space stations were basically cylinders as big as a single railway carriage with wings. The first, called Salyut 1, was launched in 1971 and was 14 m long. A new space station called Mir was launched in 1986. It is an improved Salyut cylinder, to which the Soviets

MIR (MEANING "PEACE") LAUNCHED BY USSR IN 1986, 13.5 M LONG, WEIGHT 20 T

Left: The US Skylab space station was launched in 1973 to house three astronauts. It re-entered the Earth's atmosphere in 1979.

are adding new cylindrical modules so that eventually the Mir complex will consist of five modules joined together; each module will be used for different purposes. Plans have been thwarted by technical problems and budget cuts. By 1990, when the complex was supposed to have been completed, only three new scientific modules, called Kvant, had been added.

The Russians have been able to fly crews for missions lasting one year and may fly longer missions; fresh supplies and equipment are ferried up by an unmanned tanker called Progress which is controlled from the ground. Seven cosmonauts have amassed over 300 days' spaceflight experience and one, Yuri Romanenko, has clocked up 430 days on three flights. The longest spaceflight is 365 days by Vladimir Titov and Musa Manarov in 1987-88.

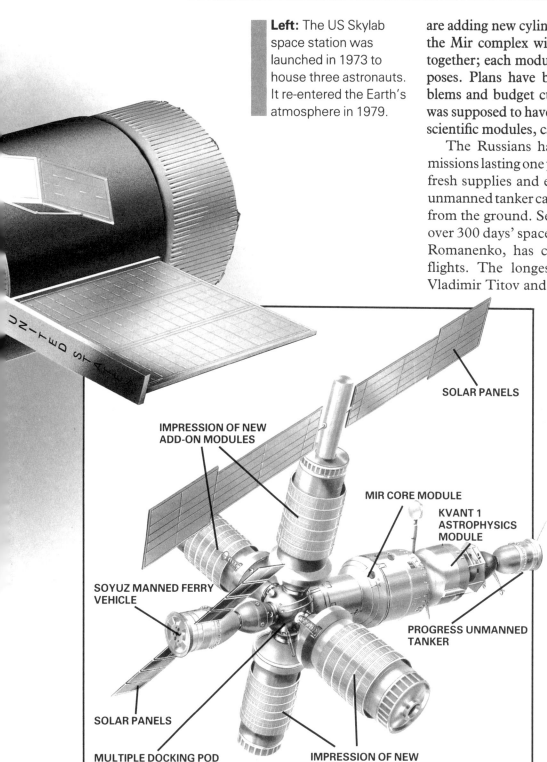

SOLAR PANELS

IMPRESSION OF NEW ADD-ON MODULES

MIR CORE MODULE

KVANT 1 ASTROPHYSICS MODULE

SOYUZ MANNED FERRY VEHICLE

PROGRESS UNMANNED TANKER

SOLAR PANELS

MULTIPLE DOCKING POD

IMPRESSION OF NEW ADD-ON MODULES

SPACE STATIONS

Salyut 1 (1971, USSR): three cosmonauts stay for record 23 days (but are killed in a re-entry accident).

Skylab (1973, USA): three crews of three astronauts each stay for record 28-, 59- and 84-day missions.

Salyut 3 (1974, USSR): first military space base.

Salyut 4 (1974, USSR): Soviets stay for 62 days.

Salyut 5 (1976, USSR): military space base

Salyut 6 (1977,USSR): crews stay for 96, 139, 175 and 184 days.

Salyut 7 (1982, USSR): flights extended to 211 and 236 days.

Mir (1986, USSR): first flight to exceed 300 days, then record 365 days.

Left: An artist's impression of the completed Soviet Mir space station complex.

SKYLAB, LARGEST SPACECRAFT EVER LAUNCHED, 35 M LONG, WEIGHT 75 T

LIVING IN SPACE

The first problem astronauts encounter when they enter space is weightlessness because of the lack of gravity. Floating around a spacecraft makes it difficult for them to work and carry out experiments, and it can make some space travellers feel sick. About half of those who travel into space feel ill for the first few days before they acclimatize to the weightlessness.

On very long journeys, it is absolutely essential that two hours each day are spent rigorously exercising. Otherwise the muscles and heart would soon weaken as they have little work to do in zero-gravity. On the Space Shuttle, astronauts jog on a treadmill wearing an elasticated harness to hold them down.

Eating, sleeping and going to the toilet are much the same as on Earth except that weightlessness has to be taken into account. Food is in small containers, so that it can be scooped out with a spoon, like ice cream from a tub. Most of the food is moist so it does not break up into crumbs that float off in the weightlessness. To sleep, the astronauts zip themselves inside sleeping bags which are attached to the bunks. The toilet has a special vacuum flush to suck the waste into a tank.

Suiting Up

While the astronauts are inside the pressurized spacecraft, they can wear casual clothes for comfort, but to work outside the spacecraft, they need space-suits. These not only provide them with oxygen under pressure, but also give protection from the dangers outside, such as the extreme heat or cold, the vacuum (lack of air), the radiation and the possible impact of micrometeorites or small pieces of space debris. Space suits are made of several layers of insulating material, with a white outer covering to reflect the Sun's rays. Under this is underwear which has tubes of water running through it to cool the astronaut. A backpack, called the portable life support system, carries oxygen and cooling water for the underwear, as well as a radio unit.

One of the newest space inventions is the manned manoeuvring unit, which enables an astronaut to fly independently using gas thrusters on the unit to move about in space. Otherwise, astronauts have to wear a safety harness when working outside the spacecraft to prevent them floating away into space.

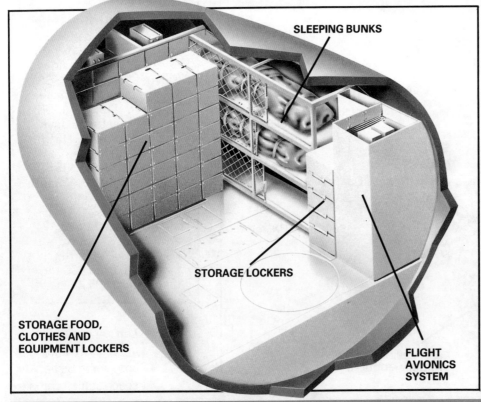

SLEEPING BUNKS

STORAGE LOCKERS

STORAGE FOOD, CLOTHES AND EQUIPMENT LOCKERS

FLIGHT AVIONICS SYSTEM

Left: Even on the Space Shuttle, living space is cramped. The lower mid-deck has to serve as a locker room, bedroom, toilet and bathroom.

Right: The first person to become an independent satellite, Bruce McCandless. In 1984, using a hand-controlled device called a manned manoeuvring unit, he flew 100 m from the Shuttle.

LONGEST MANNED SPACEFLIGHT 365 DAYS BY VLADIMIR TITOV AND MUSA MANAROV

LARGEST CREW IN SPACE IS EIGHT, ON *CHALLENGER 9* SPACE SHUTTLE, IN 1985

LIFE AMONG THE STARS

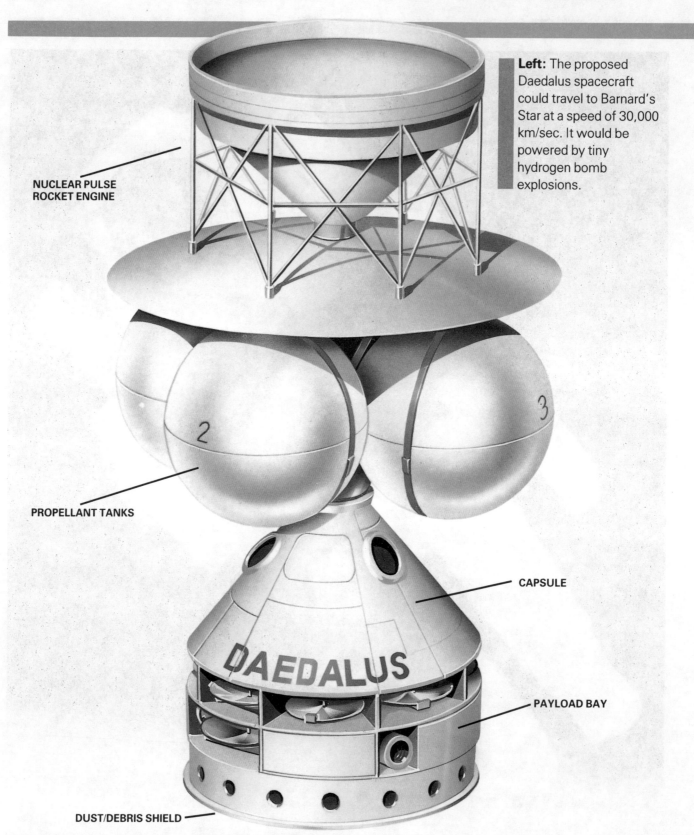

NUCLEAR PULSE ROCKET ENGINE

Left: The proposed Daedalus spacecraft could travel to Barnard's Star at a speed of 30,000 km/sec. It would be powered by tiny hydrogen bomb explosions.

PROPELLANT TANKS

CAPSULE

PAYLOAD BAY

DUST/DEBRIS SHIELD

DAEDALUS, THE FIRST STARSHIP, WILL TRAVEL AT 30,000 KM/SEC TO BARNARD'S STAR

In science fiction, spacecraft travel to planets inhabited by strange beings and establish space stations deep in space. But to do this, our spacecraft need to travel faster. The fastest spacecraft we have sent into space is Voyager 2; in 12 years it has travelled 5,000 million km. It is now on course for Sirius, which is the brightest star in our sky and also one of the closest stars to Earth, but even so is still 8.64 light years away. Voyager will pass it at a distance of 0.8 light years in just 368,000 years time!

Daedalus – The First Starship
The British Interplanetary Society have designed a starship called Daedalus. This unmanned probe will be sent on a 50-year trip to Barnard's Star. Only 5.9 light years away, it is one of the closest stars and seems to have a planetary system around it. Daedalus is 20 times the size of the Apollo Saturn V rocket and will be powered by a nuclear fission engine which will enable it to travel at 0.1 times the speed of light – 30,000 km/sec.

After reaching Barnard's Star, Daedalus will transmit data from the 450-t monitoring equipment and sensors. The spacecraft will have an enormous nuclear generator to create the power needed to send strong radio signals. These may be picked up on Earth six years later.

Searching for Other Life
Mankind has two methods of searching for possible other life in space: sending spaceprobes to the planets of our Solar System and listening with radio telescopes for possible messages from distant civilizations.

The Voyager 2 probe is carrying messages to any civilization that may one day interrupt it. In the grooves of a record are encoded written messages, pictures of our planet, spoken greetings, various sounds of life on our planet, plus some of the Earth's greatest musical hits.

Messages have also been sent into space by radio telescope. In 1974, the Arecibo radio telescope in Puerto Rico sent a message in code to a distant star cluster called M13 in the constellation of Hercules. This message from the world's largest radio telescope told aliens about our body chemistry, appearance and size, and our Solar System. The star cluster is so far away that even if any aliens there replied immediately,

we would not hear from them until AD 50000.

Some people say they have seen UFOs or unidentified flying objects, but these turn out to be bright planets and stars, aircraft, meteors and satellites.

Some people believe that God created "the Heaven and the Earth" and made life on Earth and man "in his own image". The Bible doesn't mention life on any other world in space. How do we know that there are other worlds in space capable of sustaining life? There are nine planets orbiting our Sun and none of the others can support life as we know it. Finding other worlds that may be capable of supporting lifeforms are so far away that it would take thousands of years to make contact. Today, when so many man-made satellites are constantly circling the earth, we can hardly believe that any creatures from outer space could land on Earth and leave without detection. For the time being, we must be content to look at the beautiful photographs of Earth taken by the Apollo astronauts. We need to take care of our Earth far more than we need to search for life elsewhere.

Left: An imaginary alien spaceship from another world in the Universe. Could there be life in space beyond our Solar System?

WE KNOW THERE IS NO OTHER LIFE IN OUR SOLAR SYSTEM, BUT BEYOND THIS?

IMPORTANT DATES

BC

4–3000 Chinese observe eclipses of Moon and Sun

3000 Egyptians develop astronomy as a science

600 Greek philosopher, Thales of Miletus, considers Earth may be round

500 Greeks understand phases of the Moon

400 Greek astronomer Eudoxus says Earth rotates

300 Aristarchus says Earth orbits Sun

200 Hipparchus compiles star catalogue of over 1,000 stars

AD

200 Ptolemy produces a revolutionary astronomy encyclopedia

827 Ptolemy's encyclopedia is translated into Arabic as the *Almagest*

1054 Chinese observe a supernova where the Crab nebula is today

1543 Nicolaus Copernicus says Sun is the centre of the Universe

1608 First telescope designed by Hans Lippershey

1609 First known observations using a telescope made by Galileo

1609 Johannes Kepler says that planets orbit the Sun

1666 Isaac Newton formulates laws of gravity

1668 Newton builds first reflecting telescope

1675 Speed of light measured as 299,792 km/sec

1705 Edmond Halley predicts a comet will appear in 1758. It does, and is named after him

1767 *Nautical Almanac* of heavenly bodies published

1781 Charles Messier's catalogue of nebulae and star clusters published

1781 William Herschel discovers the planet Uranus

1801 Giuseppe Piazzi discovers first asteroid, Ceres

1802 William Herschel discovers binary stars

1838 Friedrich Wilhelm Bessel measures the distance to the first star: 61 Cygni

1846 Eighth planet, Neptune, first predicted independently by John Couch Adams and Urbain Leverrier, subsequently discovered by Johann Gottfried Galle

1863 Pietro Angelo Secchi classifies stars by spectral type

1877 Giovanni Schiaparelli observes "canals" on Mars

1905 Albert Einstein announces the Theory of Relativity

1918 2.5-m reflecting telescope built on Mt Wilson, USA

1925 Edwin Powell Hubble uses 2.5-m telescope to show other galaxies are receding from us, confirming idea of expanding Universe

1930 Pluto discovered by Tombaugh

1931 Karl Jansky discovers radio waves from outer space

1937 First radio telescope built by Grote Reber

1948 5-m Palomar reflecting telescope built

1955 Jodrell Bank radio telescope built

1963 Quasars first detected

1967 Pulsars discovered

1959 Soviet Luna 2 hits Moon

1959 Luna 3 photographs far side of Moon

1962 First successful spaceprobe, Mariner 2, flies past Venus

1964 First close-up photographs of Moon

1965 Mariner 4 sends back close-up photographs of Mars

1966 Luna 9 soft lands on Moon

1966 Luna 10 orbits Moon

1966 Lunar orbiter begins Moon mapping programme

1967 Venera 4 explores atmosphere of Venus

1968 Apollo 8 orbits the Moon with three astronauts

1969 First men land on Moon in Apollo 11

1970 Venera 7 is first spacecraft to land on Venus and return data

1970 Luna 16 returns samples of Moon to Earth

1970 Luna 17 deploys unmanned lunar rover

1971 Apollo 15 astronauts drive lunar rover

1971 Mariner 9 is first spaceship to enter Mars' orbit

1972 Apollo 17 makes the final manned flight to the Moon

1973 Pioneer 10 explores Jupiter

1974 Pioneer 11 explores Saturn

1974 Mars 5 becomes only successful Soviet Mars probe

1974 Mariner 10 is first spaceprobe to explore Mercury

1975 Russian Venera 9 and Venera 10 soft land on Venus and send back first pictures from surface

1976 Vikings 1 and 2 make the first soft landings on Mars

1978 Pioneer 12 orbits Venus and deposits landers

1979 Voyager 2 flies past Jupiter

1980 Voyager 1 flies past Saturn, instruments show complex ring system

1981 Voyager 2 flies past Saturn

1982 Venera 13 returns first colour pictures from surface of Venus

1985 Vega 1 and 2 deploy balloons into atmosphere of Venus

1986 Armada of spacecraft, led by Europe's Giotto, explores Halley's Comet

1986 Voyager 2 flies by Uranus

1989 Voyager 2 flies by Neptune

1990 Japanese place lunar probe in orbit.

1990 Galileo en route to enter orbit around Jupiter and deploy atmosphere probe

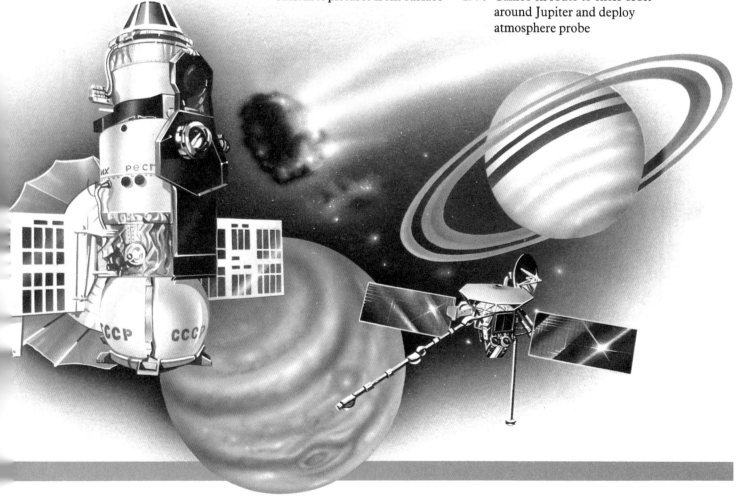

1232 China launches first rockets

1806 British soldier William Congreve launches large solid propellant rocket in battle against Boulogne

1903 Russian schoolteacher Konstantin Tsiolkovsy foresees manned space travel

1926 American physicist Robert Goddard launches first liquid propellant rocket

1943 Germany launches V2 rocket

1951 Viking 7 rocket reaches height of 200 km

1955 USA and USSR propose launches of satellites

1957 USSR launches first intercontinental ballistic missile

1957 USSR launches first satellite, Sputnik 1

1957 USSR launches dog, Laika, into orbit

1958 America launches satellite

1959 Luna 2 hits Moon

1959 First spy satellites launched

1959 Luna 3 photographs far side of Moon

1960 USA launches first weather and navigation satellites

1960 Capsule recovered from orbit by USA

1960 USSR recovers two dogs, Belka and Strelka, from orbit

1961 Yuri Gagarin in Vostok 1 is the first man to be launched into space

1961 US President John F Kennedy begins Project Apollo to put men on Moon

1962 First communications satellite, Telstar, launched

1964 Syncom 3 is the first communications satellite to be launched into geostationary orbit over the Pacific Ocean

1965 First rendezvous in space between Gemini 6, and Gemini 7, already in orbit

1966 Gemini 8 made first docking in space

1967 First flight of Saturn V booster

1968 First men orbit Moon in Apollo 8

1969 Manned lunar landing by Apollo 11

1971 USSR launches first space station, Salyut 1

1972 Pioneer 10 launched on mission to leave Solar System

1972 First Earth monitoring satellite launched

1977 Space Shuttle glide tests in atmosphere

1979 Europe launches first Ariane satellite booster

1981 First flight by Space Shuttle with Columbia orbiter

1984 First retrieval of satellites in space by Shuttle

1986 Space Shuttle Challenger explodes shortly after launch

1987 USSR launches massive Energia booster

1988 First manned spaceflight to last one year aboard Mir space station

1988 USSR launches unmanned Space Shuttle, Buran

1989 First direct broadcast TV satellites launched

1961 USSR launches Yuri Gagarin into orbit around the Earth

1961 Alan Shepard becomes first American in space

1963 Valentina Tereshkova is first woman in space

1964 USSR launches three men in Voskhod 1 to make a day-long flight

1965 Soviet Alexei Leonov becomes first spacewalker from Voskhod 2

1965 Gemini 6 makes space rendezvous with Gemini 7, already in space

1966 Gemini 8 makes first space docking

1967 Three astronauts killed in Apollo launch pad fire

1967 Vladimir Komarov killed during spaceflight of Soyuz 1

1968 Apollo 8 carries three Americans into Moon orbit

1969 Americans Neil Armstrong and Edwin (Buzz) Aldrin become first men on Moon

1970 Astronauts survive when Apollo 13 explodes en route to Moon

1971 Three Soviets aboard Soyuz 11 die during re-entry accident returning from Salyut 1 space station

1971 Dave Scott and Jim Irwin on Apollo 15 mission drive first lunar rover

1972 Apollo 17 makes last lunar landing

1973 USA's Skylab space station launched and crewed by astronauts

1973 Gerald Carr, Edward Gibson and William Pogue stay aboard Skylab for 84 days

1975 US Apollo and Soviet Soyuz dock in space and are linked together for two days

1977 Yuri Romanenko and Georgi Grechko in space for 96 days aboard Salyut 6 space station

1978 Vladimir Kovalyonok and Alexander Ivanchenkov extend space record to 139 days

1979 175-day stay by Vladimir Lyakhov and Valery Ryumin

1980 Valery Ryumin and Leonid Popov spend 185 days in Salyut 6

1981 John Young and Robert Crippen fly US Space Shuttle on its maiden flight

1982 Anatoli Berezevoi and Valentin Lebedev fly for 211 days in Salyut 7

1982 USSR launches second woman in space, Svetlana Savitskaya, to Salyut 7

1982 US Space Shuttle carries four crew

1983 Space Shuttle carries crews of five and six

1983 Soyuz T10 explodes on launch

1984 Bruce McCandless flies manned manoeuvring unit

1984 Three Soviet cosmonauts make a 236-day flight

1984 Svetlana Savitskaya becomes first female spacewalker

1984 Space Shuttles flies 100th manned spaceflight

1984 Space Shuttle carries seven crew, including two women

1985 Space Shuttle carries eight crew

1986 Space Shuttle Challenger explosion shortly after launch kills seven astronauts

1987 Yuri Romanenko flies 326-day mission on Mir space station

1988 Space Shuttle flies again

1988 Vladimir Titov and Musa Manarov complete record 365-day space mission

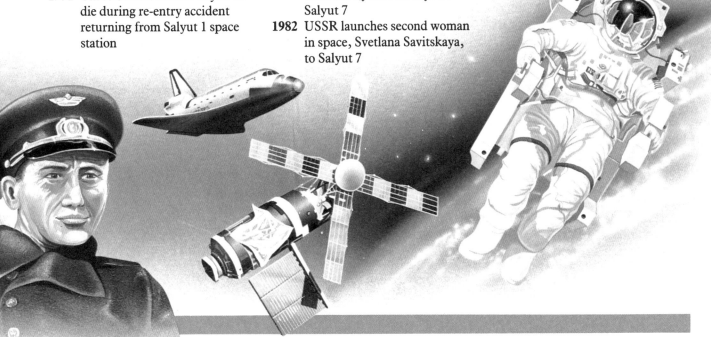

INDEX

156

INDEX

ACKNOWLEDGEMENTS

The publishers would like to thank the following organizations and individuals for their kind permission to reproduce the pictures in this book:

Aberdeen City Arts-Libraries 102; AEA Technology, Harwell 115; J. Allan Cash Photolibrary, London 83, 105 top, 107 left, 113, 119 right; Allsport/Gary Mortimore 12/Christian Petit Vandystadt 13; Ancient Art and Architecture Collection 79; Associated Press/Topham 135 top; Colorsport/Gromik Thierry 59; Daily Telegraph Colour Library 126, 135 below, 141; Dixons Ltd 109; Mary Evans Picture Library, London 88 top; Stephen Gorton 35 bottom; Michael Holford, Loughton 87 top; Hulton Picture Company 65 bottom; Hutchinson Library/Jeremy A Horner 29; Kodak Museum 99; Mansell Collection, London 112; NASA 131 top, 145, 149; Octopus Colour Picture Library/NASA 138, 139/European Space Agency 133 below/NASA 125, 128-129/US Department of Defence 134; Panos Pictures/Bruce Paton 88 bottom; QA Photos, Hythe 87 bottom; Rex Features/Sipa Press 57; Ann Ronan Picture Library, Bishops Hull 25, 39, 47, 67 bottom, 77, 79, 82, 84, 90-91, 97, 108; Science Photo Library 10, 25, 36, 37/Almos National Laboratory 53/Peter Aprahamian 17/BSIP Boucharlat 71 bottom/J L Charmet 45, 51, 67 top/CNRI 41/Martin Dohrn 32/Dr Mike McNamee 8/Peter Menzel 18/Hank Morgan 71 top/NASA 15, 23/David Parker 31, 69/STCA. Sternberg 49 bottom/Sinclair Stammers 63/St. Bartholomews Hospital 65 top/David Taylor 43/U.S. Library of Congress 33; Simon-Carves Ltd 116,117; Tony Stone Worldwide/Stephen Johnson 49 inset; TRH Pictures, London 107 right; University of Pennsylvania/Science Museum, London 49 top; John Watney Photo Library, Bowness on Solway 103; Zefa Picture Library, London 89, 105 bottom, 111, 119 left.

Ilustrations by:
David Bergen 125 top, 138, 140, 151; Wayne Ford 41, 62, 63, Ray Hutchins 84-85, 106 top; Kevin Jones (Artist Partners) 27, 76-77; Joe Lawrence 11, 16, 19, 22-23, 31, 33, 40, 48, 52, 74-75, 103, 104, 115; The Maltings Partnership 9, 13, 15,, 17, 18, 20-21, 24-25, 26, 30, 32-33, 37, 38, 44-45, 46-47, 50-51, 56-57, 58-59, 64, 69, 70 top, 77 below, 78, 82, 86, 95, 97, 98-99, 99, 100-101, 106 middle, 106-107, 108-109, 111, 113, 114, 118, 119, 130-131, 135 top, 141 top, 144-145, 149 top, 150; Finbar O'Connor 14, 39, 42, 66, 68; Mark Stacey 94, 96, 110, 120-121; Mark Summersby 70 below